RAND

Validating National Curriculum Indicators

*Leigh Burstein, Lorraine M. McDonnell,
Jeannette Van Winkle, Tor H. Ormseth,
Jim Mirocha, Gretchen Guiton*

Prepared for the
National Science Foundation

Over the past decade, education policy has focused on the teaching and learning process, prompting a variety of efforts to improve the quality of indicator data. Measures of educational resources and student achievement have traditionally received the most attention, but information on the curriculum opportunities afforded U.S. students is now generating even greater interest. Therefore, reliable procedures are needed for validating the curriculum indicator data collected from national surveys of teachers. This study was undertaken to develop and pilot a set of validation procedures to improve the quality of these data.

The study is intended to assist federal- and state-level officials responsible for designing large-scale surveys to collect data on the condition of schooling. It should also be of interest to policymakers, education professionals, and researchers concerned with measuring the opportunities provided different students to learn the academic content expected of them.

This research was supported by the National Science Foundation and the National Center for Education Statistics.

We are publishing this report with great sadness, because the first author, Leigh Burstein, died just as we began the data analysis. Leigh's entire professional career was devoted to improving the quality of educational measurement, and his special interest was measuring the curriculum experienced by students in local schools and classrooms. This study was meant to be one more step in Leigh's ongoing research; we hope others will find it sufficiently promising to build on his work.

CONTENTS

TABLES

Perhaps at no other time in the recent past have national and state education policies been so dependent on accurate information about school curriculum. Federal and state reform initiatives based on academic performance standards assume that sound indicator data are available on what students are being taught in individual schools and classrooms across the country. However, because of both its complexity and its variability, curriculum is difficult to measure. It is a multifaceted concept that includes not only the content of what is taught, but also the instructional strategies that teachers use and their goals or objectives as they present course content to students.

Most national indicators of the curriculum that students experience in American high schools are based on survey data from sources such as the National Assessment of Educational Progress (NAEP) and the National Education Longitudinal Study (NELS). Yet little effort has been devoted to validating these measures—i.e., to determining the extent to which NAEP and NELS tap what is actually taught in schools and classrooms.

STUDY PURPOSE AND METHODS

This report summarizes research aimed at improving the quality of information collected about school curriculum through surveys of classroom teachers, such as those used in NAEP and NELS. Its purpose was to design and pilot a model for collecting in-depth, benchmark data on school coursework. These data (e.g., course textbooks, assignments, exams, and teacher logs) can serve as anchors against which the validity of survey items used in national data collections might be assessed. Together, such instructional artifacts constitute a series of deeper probes than are possible with survey data, and as such, they provide a basis for assessing the extent to which survey items accurately measure the multiple dimensions of curriculum. They can also be used to monitor whether the validity of teachers' responses has been undermined by outside factors, so that reports of classroom activities are consistent with current reform rhetoric but are not matched by changes in actual practice. In-depth benchmark data are difficult and costly to collect, but they do not need to be collected as often or on as large a sample as conventional data.

In this study, homework, quizzes, classroom exercises, projects, and exams were collected over the course of a semester from a sample of 70 mathematics teachers in

California and Washington. In addition, teachers completed daily logs describing their instructional practices for five weeks, and we also obtained copies of their textbooks. These artifacts were coded to extract data about teachers' instructional activities. That information was then compared with teachers' responses on surveys similar to those administered in national data collection efforts. The objective was to ascertain whether measures of teachers' goals, activities, and content from the survey cohered or were consistent with similar measures obtained from the benchmark data. This analysis allowed us to determine how well survey data measure curriculum, as compared with data that are closer to the actual instructional process; to recommend a set of procedures for periodically validating data collected from large-scale surveys; and to suggest enhancements in the type and number of items included on those surveys.

INSTRUCTIONAL CONTENT

Our analysis suggests that curricular topics differ in the accuracy with which their coverage is reported on teacher surveys. Topics covered in upper-level courses tend to be reported with great accuracy, while those covered in lower-level courses, more general topics, topics associated with the mathematics reform movement, and those that are used as tools in the learning and application of other topics (e.g., graphing, tables and charts) are reported less accurately. We also found that although survey data may not provide a very precise picture of the amount of time spent on different topics, they reveal reasonably accurately whether a topic has been taught not at all, for only a few periods, for a week or two, or for several weeks. Given that most measures of students' opportunity-to-learn (OTL) tend to be fairly crude (typically reporting whether or not a general topic has been covered but providing no information about the time spent on it), reporting topic coverage at even this level of specificity represents a significant improvement.

Our data provide a strong rationale for including more specific curricular topics on surveys (e.g., *quadratic equations* rather than *polynomials*). Not only do they provide a more detailed and comprehensive picture of students' OTL, teachers' reports on these topics are more reliable than their reports on general topics that encompass multiple subtopics and for which it is difficult to make precise time estimates. Our artifact analysis suggests that in addition to the need for more detailed, enhanced topic lists on national surveys, validation studies are necessary to pinpoint the sources of measurement problems. For example, the lack of common agreement on the meaning of key terms associated with the mathematics reform movement (e.g., *math modeling, patterns and functions*) is likely to result in misinterpretation of data. The use of in-depth interviews and focus groups to supplement artifact analyses will help to identify the different understandings that teachers hold of concepts central to expected changes in mathematics teaching. By collecting detailed data from multiple sources over shorter periods of time (e.g., through daily logs and assignments), validation studies can provide benchmarks against which to judge the reliability of routine survey data that require teachers to recall and estimate topic coverage over longer periods of time.

INSTRUCTIONAL STRATEGY

To the extent that we were able to validate the survey data collected on teachers' instructional strategies, we found that such data present an accurate picture of the instructional strategies used most often by teachers, and they provide some indication of how teachers combine strategies during instruction. Although the picture of teaching that can be drawn from survey data is quite general, it is probably valid, because both the survey and the artifact data clearly show that there is little variation in teachers' instructional strategies. The majority of teachers use a few instructional approaches and use them often. They tend to rely most frequently on lecturing and reviewing homework and rarely, if ever, engage in activities that are consistent with the mathematics reform movement, such as student-led discussions.

The inconsistencies we identified between teachers' survey responses about the characteristics of their exams and assignments and their actual artifacts are symptomatic of a serious discrepancy. Teachers see their exams and assignments as exhibiting greater variety in their underlying instructional strategies than was evidenced in the artifact coding. They see their instruction as more varied and less traditional than is reflected in their exams and assignments, and they do not share common meanings for some of the terms used by curriculum reformers.

INSTRUCTIONAL GOALS

Our analysis suggests that instructional goals cannot be validly measured through national surveys of teachers. The data are inconsistent not only with artifact data, but also with teachers' own self-reports on other survey items such as those describing their exam formats. These inconsistencies between teachers' reports about their goal emphasis and their instructional strategies are difficult to interpret. The lack of a consistent relationship may stem from the different meanings teachers ascribe to terms associated with the mathematics reform movement. Or acknowledging the importance of particular goals may be a precursor to implementing instructional practices consistent with those objectives. Or, despite teachers' willingness to report candidly about their reliance on traditional instructional strategies, social desirability may become a factor in discussing their philosophy of teaching. These are among the many plausible explanations for the disjuncture between teachers' reported goals and classroom practice. At this point, we do not know which of these actually account for the inconsistencies, so we cannot unambiguously interpret survey data on instructional goals.

Consequently, we recommend that questions about teachers' instructional goals be deleted from national surveys. These items could be replaced with more detailed measures of topic coverage—thus improving the amount and quality of data on the most central aspect of curriculum without greatly increasing respondent burden. At least in the short term, data on teachers' goals might be more effectively gathered through smaller, supplemental studies. Data on goals might be collected as part of a validation study so that teachers' self-reports could be compared with their instructional artifacts; data might be collected in face-to-face, open-ended interviews, perhaps combined with classroom observations; or focus groups and similar strategies might be used to probe the meanings that teachers ascribe to different goals. Interpreting survey data about attitudes and beliefs is always difficult, but in the case of teachers' goals, the dangers of misinterpretation seem particularly high and appear to outweigh the value of obtaining information through a less-expensive, broad-based method.

INCORPORATING VALIDATION STUDIES INTO LARGE-SCALE SURVEYS

A validation study does not have to be conducted every time a national survey is administered. Rather, we recommend conducting one only when a new survey effort is begun—e.g., at the beginning of a longitudinal study like NELS or when major design changes are implemented in the NAEP teacher survey. A validation study would, therefore, be required for a national survey only every five years or so and would increase the cost of the survey by approximately 10 to 20 percent.

Although we recommend several modifications in the procedures used in our pilot study, we believe that the basic structure is sound. The instructional artifacts worked well as benchmarks and, despite some limitations, were easily collected from teachers. Although coding artifacts to extract information comparable to that collected from the surveys was difficult, we now have a template that can be improved upon and replicated quite easily. The coding of instructional artifacts will never be as reliable as, for example, the scoring of open-ended test items, because the type and mix of material is unstandardized across teachers. Nevertheless, we believe that high-quality benchmark data can be obtained by using survey categories as the basis for a content analysis of the artifacts and by closely monitoring the coding process.

Over the past decade, the quality of education indicators has steadily improved, particularly in indicators of school and classroom processes. The "black box" that characterized older input-output models has been replaced with an increasingly comprehensive set of indicators that can report national trends in school organization and curriculum. But the failure to validate these indicators has remained a problem. Because items are typically transferred from one survey to another with no attempts at validation, the extent to which they measure how students are actually taught is virtually unknown. This study represents a first step toward ensuring that curriculum indicators are valid and reliable measures of the instruction occurring in the nation's classrooms.

Because of the new approach to indicator design and the large volume of data associated with this project, we are indebted to a number of people with a wide variety of skills. Curtis McKnight, Andrew Porter, Senta Raizen, Stephen Weatherford, and Noreen Webb shared their methodological and substantive expertise with us at critical points during the project-design and data-analysis phases. Our project officers, Larry Suter at the National Science Foundation and Peggy Quinn at the National Center for Education Statistics, maintained their faith and support in the endeavor even when it seemed that we were lost in a maze of uninterpretable data. This report benefited from the thorough and constructive reviews of Mark Berends, Rolf Blank, and Richard Shavelson. The final product is considerably more lucid because of their efforts.

Marilyn Gerbi and Kariane Nemer organized and kept track of the thousands of pieces of artifact data that we collected and helped bring order to our sometimes chaotic enterprise. Tom Bennett, Beth Gordon, Judy Kight, John Leonard, John Novak, and Barbara Wells coded the artifact data with care and accuracy.

Despite her new responsibilities, Janet DeLand graciously volunteered to edit yet another indicator report, once again making our prose more accessible to the users as well as the producers of education indicator data.

We are particularly grateful to all the classroom teachers who provided their assignments, completed daily logs, and responded to our surveys. Their willingness to share the artifacts of their teaching made the study possible and allowed us to take one more step in learning how to measure the core activities of schooling.

Chapter One

INTRODUCTION

Efforts over the past decade to improve schooling have focused primarily on changing the way schools are governed and revising what they teach. The latter reform has been the more difficult because it is multifaceted—involving curriculum content, teacher training, instructional approaches, and student assessment—and because classroom practice has traditionally been the aspect of schooling most insulated from the reach of public policy.

The multiple dimensions of curriculum and its varied manifestations have also meant that only limited information is available about what students are being taught across the country. Although much is known about the instructional process, that understanding has typically come from in-depth studies of individual classrooms whose generalizability to a broader range of classrooms is largely unknown. Despite the growing demand for national- and state-level information about curriculum, indicator development in this area has been limited because of the difficulty of measuring complex classroom processes on a large scale. Because they are statistics that both relate to a basic construct in education and are useful in a policy context, indicators must tell a great deal about the entire system of schooling by reporting on the condition of a few of its particularly significant features. Consequently, if data on curriculum are to be used as indicators, they must measure often idiosyncratic and complex teaching activities in a consistent way across diverse classrooms and over time. They need to measure instructional activities with sufficient sensitivity to reflect what is happening in individual classrooms, but they must also produce generalizable data that can accurately describe the status of U.S. schooling.

Until recently, the general consensus has been that the measurement problems inherent in moving from in-depth descriptions of a small number of classrooms to reporting on a national sample had not been sufficiently resolved to warrant the inclusion of curriculum measures in national or state indicator systems. Yet a variety of policies, including the articulation of academic standards and new forms of student assessment, assume that information is widely available on the content and modes of instruction. In fact, most indicators of curriculum are limited to data collected by states on course offerings and enrollment, enumerated only by conventional course titles, and to national survey data based on student and teacher self-reports about coursetaking, topic coverage, and instructional strategies. Both forms of data are inadequate. Many course titles convey no information about content or how that content is presented. Although data from sources such as the National Assessment of

Educational Progress (NAEP) and the National Educational Longitudinal Study (NELS) are richer, no attempt has been made to determine whether information provided by teacher respondents is consistent with actual classroom practices and activities. Nor are any explicit design features built into national indicator efforts to monitor whether responses are being corrupted by external events.

STUDY FOCUS

The intent of this study was to develop procedures that would improve the quality of school curriculum information obtained through surveys of classroom teachers. To do this, we designed and piloted a model for collecting benchmark data on school coursework. These more in-depth data, which include course textbooks, assignments, exams, and teacher logs, can serve as anchors against which the validity of the surveys used in national data collections such as NAEP and NELS might be assessed. Together, they constitute a series of deeper probes than are possible with survey data, and they provide a basis for assessing the extent to which survey items tap what is taught in schools and classrooms. They can also be used to monitor whether the validity of teachers' responses has been undermined by outside factors—for example, reports of classroom activities may be consistent with current reform rhetoric but not matched by changes in actual practice. Benchmark data are more difficult and costly to collect than conventional survey data, but they do not need to be collected as often or on as large a sample.

We view the use of benchmark data not only as a method to measure classroom processes more accurately, but also as a way to increase the likelihood that data on curriculum will become an integral part of national and state indicator systems. The procedures outlined in this report are novel and will need to be refined through additional research and use. The difficulties inherent in measuring complex processes on a large scale remain, and throughout the report, we identify problems associated with transforming artifact data so that they can be compared with traditional survey data. Nevertheless, we believe that the innovative approach outlined here can help meet the demand for better information about how instructional approaches and curricular content vary across the country.

This study focused specifically on high school mathematics, but many of its findings apply also to other academic subjects taught in secondary schools.[1] The study design is detailed in Chapter Two, and the three subsequent chapters summarize the extent to which major dimensions of curriculum can be measured through national surveys and then validated through deeper probes in a smaller number of sites. The final chapter discusses the implications of our study for the design of future curriculum indicator systems and for the policy uses of such information. We conclude that current national indicators have significant limitations for measuring high school

---

[1]We focused on mathematics because of the interest of the National Science Foundation (NSF) in the status of the secondary mathematics curriculum. Largely because of NSF's support of past research, indicator development in this area is considerably more advanced than in other subject areas, such as social studies and language arts. Consequently, this focus provided us with a more solid base for devising methods to improve the quality of curricular data.

mathematics teaching. Although enhancing existing surveys will greatly improve those indicators, their use for more than informational purposes would be ill-advised at this time.

Before turning to a description of our research methods, we provide some background for the study by discussing the research base on which it draws and the relevant policy and practice context.

RESEARCH BASE

A growing body of research documents the relationship between student achievement, the types of courses taken, and the content and level of those courses. Some of the most compelling evidence about the relationship between achievement and curricular content comes from the Second International Mathematics Study (SIMS), conducted between 1976 and 1982.[2] As their predecessors had recognized some twenty years earlier in the First International Mathematics Survey, the SIMS researchers understood that curricular differences had to be taken into consideration when comparing student achievement across different national systems. That recognition led to the notion of opportunity-to-learn (OTL). OTL became a measure of "whether or not . . . students have had an opportunity to study a particular topic or learn how to solve a particular type of problem presented by the test" (Husen, as cited in Burstein, 1993: xxxiii). The SIMS researchers conceptualized the mathematics curriculum as functioning at three levels:

1. The *intended curriculum* as articulated by officials at the system or national level.

2. The *implemented curriculum* as interpreted by teachers in individual classrooms.

3. The *attained curriculum* as evidenced by student achievement on standardized tests and by their attitudes (Travers, 1993: 4).

The major vehicle for measuring the implemented curriculum was an OTL questionnaire administered to the teachers of tested students. Teachers were asked whether the content that would enable their students to respond to items on the achievement tests had been taught to them. They were also asked more general questions about their instructional goals, their attitudes and beliefs about mathematics teaching, their instructional strategies, and their professional backgrounds.

One of the most important purposes that SIMS served was to document differences in curriculum, and hence in opportunities to learn, across national systems. SIMS researchers found striking differences between the ways curricula are organized in

---

[2]SIMS data collection included the administration of achievement tests and questionnaires to over 125,000 students in 20 systems. Students were sampled from two population groups: Population A, consisting of students in the grade level where the majority would be 13 years of age, and Population B, consisting of all students in the terminal grade of secondary education who were also studying mathematics. In addition, supporting questionnaire data were collected from the approximately 6,000 teachers of these students and 4,000 principals or heads of mathematics departments. Information about the implemented curriculum was collected from national committees that included mathematics educators and researchers (Travers et al., 1988).

the countries where students scored highest on the SIMS tests and the way they are organized in the United States. At the lower-secondary level, the Japanese curriculum emphasizes algebra; the curricula in France and Belgium are dominated by geometry and fractions. In contrast, U.S. schools allocate their curricula more equally across a variety of topics, thus covering each subject much more superficially. The mathematics curriculum in U.S. schools is characterized by extensive repetition and review and little intensity of coverage. This low-intensity coverage means that individual topics are treated in only a few class periods, and concepts and topics are quite fragmented (McKnight et al., 1987).

The SIMS data also illustrated variations in OTL within the same national system. For example, Japan's OTL ratings for algebra content were quite similar across classrooms and teachers, ranging from 60 to 100 percent coverage of the content included in the SIMS tests, with a median topic coverage of 85 percent. In contrast, the United States' OTL ratings ranged from 0 to 100 percent, with a median of 75 percent of the SIMS topics. About 10 percent of the thirteen-year-olds tested in the United States were receiving virtually no instruction in algebra topics, and 25 percent were receiving instruction in only about half the mathematics content covered on the algebra subtest (Schmidt et al., 1993).[3] Part of the reason for the greater variation in OTL in the United States is that schools typically assign students to different kinds of mathematics classes according to their purported abilities and interests. Using the SIMS data, Kifer (1993) found that when sampled U.S. eighth-grade mathematics classes were categorized as remedial, regular, enriched, and algebra, significant differences were evident in students' opportunities to learn the content tested in SIMS. With the exception of arithmetic topics, students in remedial classes receive very little teaching on mathematics content, and even students in regular classes receive less content coverage in algebra and geometry topics than do those in enriched and algebra classes.

The SIMS results visibly influenced public discussion because they showed significant gaps in U.S. students' achievement, as compared with students in other industrialized countries. But other studies that focused solely on the United States produced similar findings about the effects of curricular exposure. For example, Raizen and Jones (1985) summarized four studies based on nationally representative student samples that showed a strong correlation between the number of mathematics courses students take and their achievement in mathematics. These relationships persist even when background variables such as home and community environment and previous mathematics learning are taken into account. Research had also shown that the level, as well as the number, of courses students take is correlated with achievement. Jones et al. (1986), after controlling for socioeconomic status and test scores achieved two years earlier, found that students in the High School and Beyond (HS&B) sample with at least five transcript credits in mathematics at or above the algebra I level scored an average of 17 percentage points higher on a standardized mathematics test than those with no course credits in higher-level mathematics. By

---

[3]On the whole, OTL was considerably more uniform in France and Japan than in the United States and New Zealand, although within-system variation is greater in all systems for geometry than for either algebra or arithmetic topics (Schmidt et al., 1993).

showing that curricular exposure is critically related to student achievement and to differences in students' learning opportunities, all these studies make a strong case for supplementing data on student achievement with information about the curriculum they experience.

POLICY AND PRACTICE CONTEXT

Growing concern about the achievement of U.S. students and the distribution of that achievement across different types of students has also prompted intensified interest in school curriculum as a focal point for policy interventions. Beginning in the mid-1980s, elected officials, especially at the state level, extended their traditional concern about how schools are governed and financed to include what schools teach, who teaches it, and in some cases, how it is taught. In fashioning policies in this area, policymakers drew on the research that demonstrated the close link between students' curricular exposure and their achievement, and on expert advice about what constitutes an engaging, productive curriculum.

Recent examples of this focus are the federal Goals 2000 legislation and similar standards-setting exercises in the states. Goals 2000 provides grants to states as inducements to establish curriculum and student-performance standards, as well as standards or strategies to ensure that students will have an opportunity to learn the content embodied in the state standards (Riley, 1994; Smith and Scoll, 1995). Even prior to the federal effort, however, a number of states were already using curriculum as a reform vehicle by relying on such strategies as the development of curricular standards and frameworks, the redesign of assessment systems, and revision of textbook adoption policies.

These federal and state initiatives have drawn on prior standards-setting efforts undertaken by professional organizations and have also prompted other disciplines to begin similar exercises. The National Council of Teachers of Mathematics (NCTM, 1989, 1991) undertook one of the earliest professional efforts to improve classroom practice through the promulgation of curricular and teaching standards. Its approach was later reflected in new state curriculum frameworks, such as those in California (California Department of Education, 1992). In mathematics, curriculum reform has been characterized by the adoption of learning goals that emphasize understanding the conceptual basis of mathematics, reasoning mathematically and applying that reasoning in everyday situations, offering alternative solutions to problems, and communicating about mathematical concepts in meaningful and useful ways. Consistent with those goals, curriculum reformers have advocated changes in both mathematics content and instructional strategies. Particularly prominent in this reform vision of the mathematics curriculum is a changed view of the teacher's role. Because students are expected to play an active part in constructing and applying mathematical ideas, teachers should be facilitators of learning rather than imparters of information. In terms of actual instructional activities, this shift means that rather than lecturing and relying on a textbook, teachers are to select and structure mathematical tasks that allow students to learn through discussion, group activities, and other modes of discovery.

Despite its growing popularity, the use of curriculum as a lever for educational reform is not without its problems. Most of the attention thus far has focused on the political difficulties inherent in defining what should be included in state curriculum standards. The recent experience of states like California, Kentucky, and Pennsylvania, where serious controversies have erupted over the content of state curriculum frameworks and assessments, illustrates the passion that can be engendered by questions about what students should be taught (Merl, 1994; Harp, 1994; Ravitch, 1995). Debate has also arisen over the use of OTL standards as part of a curricular reform strategy, with the controversy focused on values such as how equity is defined and the appropriate roles of state and local governments (National Council on Education Standards and Testing, 1992; O'Day and Smith, 1993; Rothman, 1993; Owens, 1994; Goodling, 1994).

Equally important, however, are the technical feasibility issues inherent in the use of curriculum as the focus of policy. One major problem stems from limitations on the amount and type of indicator data currently collected by the federal government and the states. Statistical data about the condition of schooling has historically focused on inputs such as per-pupil spending and outcomes, most notably student test scores. Information about how schools are organized and how students are taught has tended to be available only through studies based on data collected from limited samples on a nonroutine basis.

However, beginning in the mid-1980s, a number of researchers and policymakers began to advocate expanding the types of indicator data that were routinely collected and reported (Murnane and Raizen, 1988; Shavelson et al., 1987; 1989; OERI State Accountability Study Group, 1988; National Study Panel on Education Indicators, 1991; Porter, 1991). They argued that indicator data on school and classroom processes were necessary to monitor educational trends, to compare schooling conditions across different kinds of students in different geographic locations, and to generate information that could be used in holding schools accountable. A good part of the rationale for collecting more than just input and outcome data lay in the fact that these indicators were to be used for policy purposes. Knowing that educational conditions were getting better or worse provided little insight into why particular trends existed or how to fix problems or replicate successes. Furthermore, it had become clear that the way in which educational inputs were used was as important as the absolute level of those inputs. To accommodate the information needs of policymakers, then, it was necessary for indicator systems to include data that could provide a comprehensive picture of the schooling process as it occurred in schools and classrooms.

Consequently, proposed designs for new indicator systems advocated including process measures such as teacher background and experience, school- and grade-level organization, course offerings and student coursetaking patterns, curriculum content, availability and usage of instructional materials, and instructional strategies. In recommending that a broad array of school and classroom process measures be included in indicator systems, researchers drew upon studies documenting the relationship between student achievement and the type of instruction students receive (Shavelson et al., 1989).

Some indicator systems were expanded to include school process data. For example, at the national level, NAEP and the longitudinal surveys of students sponsored by the National Center for Education Statistics (NCES) (e.g., HS&B, NELS) collected data from students, teachers, and school administrators about school organization and resources, teacher qualifications, curricular content, and instructional strategies. These data could be disaggregated by gender, ethnicity, urbanicity, and in some cases, by state. In addition, 47 states were reporting data to the Council of Chief State School Officers on mathematics and science teacher qualifications and student coursetaking patterns (Blank and Gruebel, 1993). By 1994, 48 states were producing some type of accountability or indicator reports containing data on such factors as student test scores, attendance, and dropout rates. About half the states now issue "school report cards," which include school process data such as the proportion of students taking college preparatory or Advanced Placement (AP) courses (Council of Chief State School Officers, 1994). Although information about teacher qualifications is not typically reported by school, many states also collect such data, which could be disaggregated to the school level.

No one, however, is collecting data on the curricular content and instructional strategies available to students in different local jurisdictions. At this point, it is possible to describe how curricular opportunities differ for boys and girls, for different ethnic groups, and for urban students as compared with those in either rural or suburban areas. But we do not know whether the curriculum experienced by students in Seattle is significantly different from that of students in Chicago or Visalia, California, or whether curriculum differs greatly among schools within the same state.

In addition to these limits on the amount and type of curriculum indicator data, the available data present substantial methodological problems. Most of the data available on a school-by-school basis are derived from reports by principals and teachers about course offerings and student enrollment in those courses. However, the SIMS data suggest that because of significant variation in the breadth and depth of topic coverage, knowing that most ninth graders take algebra does not provide adequate information about their actual opportunities to learn algebra content.

Even the more comprehensive data about classroom processes collected from nationally representative samples of teachers are limited in their ability to portray a valid picture of the schooling process. Most curriculum data are collected through teacher surveys because these are cost-effective and impose only a modest time burden on respondents. However, some aspects of curricular practice simply cannot be measured without actually going into the classroom and observing the interactions between teachers and students. These interactions include discourse practices that evidence the extent of students' participation and their role in the learning process, the specific uses of small-group work, the relative emphasis placed on different topics within a lesson, and the coherence of teachers' presentations. Given the rudimentary status of curriculum data in most national and state indicator systems, efforts to obtain an accurate picture of how opportunities to learn vary for different groups of students will most likely continue to focus on a more general level than these finely grained aspects of instruction.

If policymakers and the public are interested in data about school curriculum that are both comparable across local jurisdictions and can be disaggregated to the school level, teacher surveys will remain the most feasible way to collect such information for the foreseeable future. Yet, at this point, none of the national survey data collected from teachers have been validated to determine whether they measure what is actually occurring in classrooms. Despite major advances in the design of background and school process measures, studies have generally developed only a few new items and then "borrowed" others from earlier studies. Little effort has been made to validate these measures by comparing the information they generate with that obtained through alternative measures and data collection procedures. For example, are teachers' reports of curricular goals or content coverage consistent with the material tested and the types of questions the teachers ask on their examinations?

Given the complexity of the teaching and learning process, the amount of variation across classrooms (as evidenced from more in-depth, school-based research), and shifting modes of instruction as new curricular reforms are introduced, it is reasonable to assume that surveys alone may not adequately measure even the most generic forms of instructional practice. Therefore, if teacher surveys are to remain the major source of information about the instruction that American students are receiving and if policy decisions continue to be made based on the data they provide, mechanisms will need to be established to validate the survey data. The benchmarking strategy outlined in this study, which relies on other data such as textbooks and teacher assignments, is one method for improving the quality of national and state curriculum indicator data.

Past research on the relationship between student achievement and the instruction the students receive, as well as the growing emphasis on curriculum as a policy lever, suggest several factors that need to be considered in efforts to improve the quality of curriculum indicator data. Curriculum is a multidimensional concept that includes, but is not limited to, the content of instruction. Consequently, in addition to content or topic coverage, information must be collected on teachers' instructional strategies and goals. Key elements of instructional strategy include the manner in which content is sequenced and the mode in which teachers and textbooks present it to students. For example, the effect on student learning might be quite different if a teacher presents new content through a lecture than if he or she introduces students to the same content by asking them to apply previously learned concepts to a new situation while working in small groups. Another critical dimension of curriculum consists of the goals that teachers pursue as they present course content to students. The relative emphasis that teachers give to different objectives reveals something about their expectations for a particular course, and their choice of objectives is likely to influence how they configure topics and instructional activities within that course. However, teachers' reports of their course objectives reflect intended behavior and are likely to be less reliable than reports of actual behavior, such as topic coverage and instructional activities. For that reason, data on teacher goals can be suggestive, but they must be interpreted in tandem with other information about classroom activities.

In addition, curriculum indicators need to capture the variability inherent in a complex activity such as teaching. We have noted that data on course enrollments alone are insufficient because they convey little information about the actual content of the courses and even less about the instructional strategies used. Similarly, because of the current flux in instructional policy and practice, data collection instruments need to measure both traditional forms of instruction and the newer approaches advocated by curriculum reformers. Strategies such as having students work in small groups to find joint solutions or use manipulatives to demonstrate a concept are currently much in vogue among reformers. Yet decades of research on educational change, and most recently on the implementation of curriculum reforms (e.g., Cohen and Peterson, 1990), suggest that many teachers will continue to use more traditional approaches, such as lecturing to their students and having them work exercises from a textbook. Therefore, data collection instruments need to be broadly focused and sensitive enough to reflect the diversity of classroom practice during a transitional period in school curriculum.

In the next chapter, we outline our study methods and indicate how we attempted to take past research and the current context into consideration in designing our model.

Chapter Two

STUDY METHODS

GENERAL APPROACH AND RATIONALE

Validation of survey items to ensure that they accurately measure what is happening in classrooms could be approached in a number of ways. In choosing among possible strategies, two criteria must be considered: A validation strategy should measure curricular goals, content, and instructional activities as sensitively as possible; and it must do so cost-efficiently without imposing a significant burden on teachers and students.

The methodology of teaching and learning research would suggest that detailed classroom observations provide the best information from which to make inferences about the curriculum students are actually receiving (for a detailed discussion of various approaches to teaching and learning research, see Wittrock, 1985). However, as a means of validating national indicators, this approach is problematic.

Although classroom observation is effective for capturing curricular depth, it is considerably less efficient in measuring breadth—a requirement for indicator purposes. For example, if one's purpose were to focus intently on a narrow slice of curriculum (e.g., the teaching of the Pythagorean theorem) taught at a prescribed point in most classrooms of a given course, one could target a specific amount of observation time to capture the teaching of that topic, and comparing survey responses with observational data would presumably be straightforward. But for most purposes, the span of curriculum to be measured through indicator data is much more extensive, and the sequencing of topics and time allocations varies considerably from section to section of even the same course, let alone across courses. Instruction on certain topics may also cycle throughout a course, making the targeting of observations even more impractical. Choosing a fixed time of the school year to conduct observations and capture whatever topics might be taught at that time runs the risk of misspecifying the place within a particular teacher's curriculum where the observed topic falls, as well as missing what was covered previously and planned for later. Consequently, only general survey questions dealing with activities and process, as distinct from content, could be validated in this way.

Such limitations led us to conclude that on cost and feasibility grounds alone, classroom observation, although it is an appropriate and necessary strategy for basic research on school curriculum, is not a viable tool for obtaining ongoing benchmark data. Moreover, observations that are not long-term and extensive could very well distort decisions about the validity of specific survey alternatives.

Consequently, we decided to build on prior research (McDonnell et al., 1990) and make the collection and analysis of a representative sample of teacher assignments (homework, quizzes, classroom exercises, projects, examinations), gathered throughout a semester, the centerpiece of the benchmarking effort. We believe that these examples of classwork and how the teacher uses them represent much of the curriculum as experienced by students. Thus these systematic artifacts of learning, placed within the context of syllabi and textbook coverage, constitute a solid basis for characterizing the implemented curriculum presented to students.[1] In addition, spreading data collection over a broader period of time, at a much lower cost than equivalent observational activities, considerably expands the span of curriculum that can be measured.

In this study, then, we used these instructional artifacts as deeper probes about the nature of instruction in a small number of sites. The artifacts were coded to extract data about teachers' instructional content, activities, and goals. That information was then compared with the teachers' responses on surveys similar to those administered as part of national data collection efforts.[2] The overarching question was whether measures of goals, activities, and content from the survey cohered or were correlated with similar measures obtained from the benchmark data. To the extent that inconsistencies emerged, we needed to analyze the reasons for such inconsistencies and identify ways to improve coherence in future indicator data. This produced three results: an analysis of how well survey data measure curriculum, as compared with data that are closer to the actual instructional process; a recommended set of procedures for periodically validating data collected from large-scale surveys; and suggested enhancements in the type and number of items to be included on these surveys.

STUDY SAMPLE

This study is based on data collected from a sample of 70 teachers who comprise the majority of the mathematics faculty in nine secondary schools in California and

---

[1]However, these artifacts do not provide information about how students receive and respond to the curriculum, only about how teachers present it. In our pilot study, we asked teachers, for each major assignment provided, to include two samples of student work graded A, two B/Cs, and two samples of below-C work. However, that request created an extra burden for respondents (even when arrangements were made to have the student work copied for teachers), and most of the nonresponse rate for the study was attributable to this request. Therefore, we did not request student work from the remainder of the teachers in the sample.

In the future, requests for student work may become less burdensome and intrusive as more schools adopt student portfolios and routines are established for the systematic production, copying, and storage of student work.

[2]The artifacts were coded by six experienced mathematics teachers and two project staff, using a coding instrument that paralleled the items on the survey. The coding process is described later in this chapter.

Washington.[3] The characteristics of the schools and the teachers are summarized in Table 2.1.[4]

Although the depth and exploratory nature of the data collection meant that only a small sample of teachers could be studied, we wanted to make certain that they were typical of those who participate in large national surveys. Therefore, schools were selected from among those that were part of the 1992 NELS Second Follow-up Study (NELS-SFU). Because NELS was designed to obtain data on a nationally representa-

Table 2.1

Study Sample

Sample Characteristics	Value
Number of schools	
California	
Urban	4
Suburban	1
Rural	1
Washington	
Urban	1
Suburban	2
Total	9
Mathematics classes in each of the course categories examined	
Below algebra I	20
Algebra I	15
Geometry	12
Algebra II/trigonometry	8
Math analysis/pre-calculus	7
Calculus	8
Total classes	70
Teacher characteristics	
Number of teachers	70[a]
Percent male	58
Percent female	42
Percent with college major in mathematics	47
Mean years of teaching experience (S.D. = 9)	17

[a]74 teachers agreed to participate in the study, but four dropped out before the artifact data collection was completed.

---

[3]Up to eight teachers were selected in each school. In schools where the mathematics faculty numbered more than eight, the teachers eliminated from the sample were those teaching lower-level courses (i.e., at or below algebra I), because these courses were adequately represented in our sample and we wanted to be certain also to include a sufficient number of upper-level courses.

[4]In addition to the mathematics teachers who provided data, 18 science teachers from seven of the sampled schools also participated in the study as part of an exploratory analysis for developing curriculum indicators for high school science courses. However, this report considers only the data collected from the mathematics teachers.

Each participating teacher was paid an honorarium of $175 to complete two surveys and provide instructional artifacts over the course of a semester. The 13 teachers who participated in follow-up interviews were paid an additional $50 each.

tive sample of students, teachers were included only if they taught students in that sample. Therefore, the 2,606 mathematics teachers surveyed in NELS-SFU do not constitute a nationally representative sample of high school mathematics teachers. However, to evaluate how our much smaller sample compares with a larger one drawn from across the country, we compared our teachers with the NELS-SFU sample and found that the mean years of teaching experience was exactly the same for the two groups. Our sample had a slightly higher proportion of males (58 percent, compared with 52 percent for NELS-SFU), but the major difference between the two groups was that our sample included a considerably lower proportion of teachers with a college major in mathematics (47 percent, compared with 70 percent in the NELS-SFU sample).

Twenty-four schools were contacted, and 13 agreed to participate. Nine declined to participate, and four of those that agreed were eliminated for various reasons, such as having very small mathematics faculties or year-round schedules that did not coincide with our data collection timetable.

Five of the nine participating schools are located in urban areas, three are suburban, and one is rural. The largest school enrolls 2,800 students, but five schools have enrollments in excess of 2,000. The smallest school enrolls 980 students. In five of the schools, 65 percent or more of the students are white, while the other four have minority enrollments of 65 percent or more.

DATA

Table 2.2 summarizes the types of data collected and the purpose each data source served in the study design. All the data are discussed at greater length below.

Teacher Surveys

Three factors shaped the design and administration of the survey component of the study. First, because the purpose of the project was to validate data collected as part of efforts such as NELS, the survey instrument needed to approximate closely the type administered in national surveys. Second, we had to make certain that the collection of artifact data did not bias teachers' survey responses by sensitizing them to the kinds of questions that would later be asked of them on the survey.[5] Finally, we wanted to pilot the administration of a more extensive survey than has typically been used in national indicator data collection.

---

[5]Our concerns about artifact data collection contaminating survey responses were twofold: First, we were concerned that if teachers were completing daily logs and providing assignments throughout the semester, they might become more aware of the types and frequency of their classroom activities than they would ordinarily be. Consequently, their survey responses would be more accurate than would be the case in routine data collection when teachers only complete a survey. If that were the case, the survey responses in our study would not be equivalent to those collected in national indicator efforts. Second, we were concerned that because of their direct contact with members of the research team throughout the semester, teachers might be more likely to give what they considered to be socially desirable responses. In this case, those responses were likely to be consistent with the rhetoric of the mathematics reform movement and away from more traditional teaching strategies.

Table 2.2

Study Data

Type of Data	Purpose
Survey (administered *prior* to artifact data collection)	• Obtain teacher self-reports about topic coverage, instructional strategies, and goals on a survey instrument analogous to the format and level of detail on national surveys. Data also collected on teacher background and experience.
	• Serve as a basis for gauging the extent to which teachers' responses were altered by the artifact data collection.
Survey (administered *after* artifact data collection)[a]	• Obtain more extensive teacher self-reports with a more detailed list of topics, instructional activities, and goals and with items that tap these dimensions in multiple ways.
Course textbooks	• Validate survey data on topic coverage.
Teacher daily logs (5 weeks)	• Obtain more precise self-reports from teachers on topic coverage and instructional activities.
Daily assignments (5 weeks)	• Validate survey data on topic coverage, goals, and instructional strategies (viz., assignment/exam format and characteristics).
Exams and quizzes (5 weeks)	
Major assignments and projects (entire semester)	
Interviews with principals, counselors, and mathematics department chairs	• Obtain information on school context—student characteristics, the different levels of courses offered, and how teachers and students are assigned to courses.
Follow-up group interviews[b]	• Identify reasons for anomalous findings.

[a]86 percent of the sample completed both the pre– and post–data-collection samples. The remainder completed one of the two surveys.
[b]Thirteen teachers from two of the schools participated in the follow-up group interviews.

Our strategy for taking these factors into consideration was to administer a survey prior to collecting the artifact data. This survey included the same items as those in the sections on instructional activities, content, goals, and teacher background in the teacher questionnaire administered as part of the 1992 NELS-SFU. Teachers were asked to respond in terms of one particular section of a single course that they were teaching. We then collected artifact data on that same section over one semester.

At the end of the semester, after the artifact data had been collected, we administered a second survey that repeated the same instructional activities and content items asked on the first survey but also included an expanded list of topics, goals, and instructional activities. The NELS-SFU survey contained 11 items to measure content coverage, 16 items on instructional strategies, and 10 on goals and objectives. In contrast, the survey we administered after the artifact data collection included 30 items that measured content coverage (with a separate topic list for courses at or above the algebra II level and another for courses below that level), 33 items on instructional strategies, and 32 on goals and objectives. The enhanced survey also included items designed to measure teachers' expectations about levels of student understanding and their conceptions of their role in student learning. Both questionnaires are reproduced in the Appendix.

In addition to expanding the second survey to probe in greater depth and to measure curriculum in more diverse ways, we also experimented with a variety of different item formats and response options. For example, the NELS survey asks teachers whether a topic was *taught previously, reviewed only, taught as new content, will be taught or reviewed later in the year*, or *is beyond the scope of the course or not included in the curriculum*. In addition to this response option, the enhanced survey also asked about the number of periods spent on a topic, using a response option that included six categories ranging from *0 periods* to *>20 periods*. In some questions, teachers were asked to describe the percentage of class time or of an assignment devoted to instructional activities; responses were elicited in some cases as a continuous variable, and in others as a categorical variable. In other questions, frequency was defined as a categorical measure ranging from *almost every day* to *never*. Similarly, teachers were asked about the amount of emphasis they give to different goals, but they were also asked about curricular goals more indirectly in a question that probed their expectations for students' level of understanding. Including a variety of different types of response options provided us with another source of information on which to base recommendations about how to improve existing surveys.

Analysis of the two surveys suggests that teachers' responses were not biased by the artifact data collection and that validation procedures can be designed to be implemented either before or after survey data have been collected. When we compared teachers' responses to the two surveys, we found few significant differences between their responses on items that appeared on both. On average, across all items common to both surveys, 90 percent differed by no more than one response option, and 60 percent were exactly the same on the two surveys. Those items for which a large proportion of responses changed were those that would be expected to change between the beginning and end of the semester because teachers have more precise information at the end—e.g., the percentage of class time spent administering tests or quizzes, the frequency of teacher-led discussions. In addition, there was no evidence that teachers gave socially desirable responses or felt it necessary to present an image of their teaching that was consistent with the rhetoric of the mathematics reform movement. As the discussion in the subsequent chapters will indicate, a large proportion of teachers reported engaging in traditional activities such as lecturing and correcting or reviewing homework on a daily basis, and most teachers engaged in reform-oriented activities such as student-led discussions rarely or not at all.

Instructional Artifacts

Course textbooks. A copy of the textbook used by each teacher in the study sample was purchased, and teachers were asked on the post–artifact-data-collection survey which chapters they had covered over the course of the semester and which additional ones they had already covered or planned to cover during the rest of the year.[6] All the chapters or lessons a teacher reported as covering were then coded to determine which topics were covered. That information became one of the benchmarks against which topic coverage, as reported by teachers on the survey, was compared.

Teacher daily logs. During the same five weeks that all their daily assignments were collected, teachers were also asked to complete a one-page log form (included in the Appendix) at the end of each day. The form asked them to list which topics they covered during that day's class period and to indicate on a checklist all the modes of instruction they used and the activities in which the students engaged. There was also a *comments* section where teachers were asked to provide any information about the lesson that they felt was important (e.g., that class time was reduced by other school activities, that something particularly different or innovative occurred that day). To minimize teacher burden, the log form was designed to be completed in approximately 5 minutes.

Because the logs were completed by teachers, they do not constitute an external source for validating the surveys in the same way that textbooks and assignments do. However, they do serve as a check on the reliability of the surveys, since they provide greater detail about classroom activities, with the information collected closer in time to the actual events.

Assignments. Teachers were asked to provide copies of every assignment they gave to students for a period of five weeks. The five weeks were divided into one week at the beginning of the semester, three consecutive weeks in the middle, and one week at the end. During these times, teachers provided all in-class and homework assignments, quizzes, exams, major projects, and any other written work assigned to students. In addition, teachers completed a preprinted label, checking the major purpose of each assignment given, its relationship to other classwork, whether the work was done individually or in groups, and whether it was done inside or outside the classroom. This label was affixed to each assignment. During the remaining weeks of the semester, teachers provided copies of their major assignments only— i.e., exams, papers more than three pages in length, and projects. A preprinted label was also attached to each of these assignments. On average, 20 assignments, including major assignments and projects, were provided by each participating teacher (n = 1,407). Each teacher administered an average of five exams and quizzes (n = 368).

Interviews

In each school, we conducted face-to-face interviews with the principal, the head counselor, and the mathematics department chair. These interviews were, on average, about 45 minutes long and focused on the type of students attending the school,

---

[6]Four teachers did not use a textbook. Two teach interactive mathematics, which is an alternative method for teaching algebra and geometry that combines the two subjects and integrates individual topics within a problem-solving focus. The other two teach mathematics A-B, a course offered in California schools for those students who need to take a preparatory course prior to beginning algebra. One other teacher in the sample used a textbook published more than ten years ago that is now out of print. Consequently, this data source was not available for five teachers.

the different levels of courses offered, the criteria the school used in assigning students to different mathematics courses and sections, and how decisions about teacher assignments were made. We also asked the department chairs to describe in some detail the major differences among the mathematics courses offered by the school in terms of level of difficulty, types of students enrolled, topics covered, instructional materials and strategies, course requirements, and grading practices. These interviews helped us place the survey and artifact data in a richer and more valid context. We were particularly interested in finding out whether there were any recent school- or department-level initiatives that might be shaping the curricular content or instructional approaches used by teachers.

We had not planned to conduct any follow-up interviews with teachers after the artifact data were collected. However, we had difficulty interpreting several key findings that showed a lack of internal consistency between what teachers reported on the survey as their goals and what they reported about instructional activities. We found, for example, that a substantial proportion (40 percent) of teachers reported a *major* or *moderate* emphasis on most of the goals consistent with the mathematics reform movement. However, only a small proportion (12 percent) reported engaging regularly in most of the instructional activities advocated by the NCTM. Similarly, the mean level of agreement between teachers' self-reports about their goals on the surveys and the coding of their exams was low. The typical pattern was for teachers to report a *minor* or *moderate* emphasis on most goals, while coders judged teachers' exams as showing *no* emphasis on those goals. The discrepancy was greatest on the so-called "reform" goals and considerably less on more traditional goals (e.g., performing calculations with speed and accuracy).

Before we concluded that these discrepancies represented "real" differences between teachers' reported and actual behaviors, we wanted to make certain that they were not the result of fundamental differences between teachers' interpretations of survey items and those of the coders who were using the reform movement's definitions. We decided to address these questions through the use of follow-up group interviews. We interviewed all the original study participants from two high schools in several group discussions that lasted about 90 minutes each. We asked teachers questions that would help us clarify our anomalous results. For example, with regard to the instructional goals that seemed to have been interpreted inconsistently, we asked: "In the course you reported on in your survey, what types of instructional activities do you see as representing this particular goal?" We present the results of these group interviews in subsequent chapters of this report as one basis for interpreting some of our findings.

The study data were collected in four waves. We initially collected data from teachers in two schools in the spring of 1992, as a pilot for the rest of the study. We found no substantive problems with our data collection instruments and procedures, but we needed to streamline them to reduce teacher burden. Consequently, the request for graded student work was eliminated and the enhanced teacher survey was shortened. We also wanted to make certain that there would be no significant differences between collecting data in the fall semester and collecting them in the spring semester. Therefore, we collected data from three additional schools in fall 1992 and from the remaining four in spring 1993. The follow-up group interviews were conducted in March 1994.

CODING THE ARTIFACT DATA

The effectiveness of a validation strategy based on instructional artifacts rests entirely on how information is coded or extracted from those artifacts. Valid and reliable coding requires that three criteria be met: First, to make comparisons between the survey and the artifacts, the coding format needs to parallel the survey items as closely as possible. In addition to a similar format for the two types of data, the survey items and the coding categories must be so clearly defined that teachers and coders will interpret them similarly. Second, the coding should extract as much information as possible from the artifacts, but it needs to do so without requiring judgments or inferences that go beyond the data. Third, the data must be coded reliably, i.e., another coder would make the same judgments about the same information.

Several factors work against meeting these criteria, however. First, artifact data are unstandardized—the type and mix of assignments can vary considerably across teachers. Even the textbooks in our sample, the most standardized type of artifact, varied from the conventional (e.g., Dolciani's algebra I text) to the innovative (e.g., Sunburst Geometry, Merrill's integrated math series) to the controversial (the Saxon series).

Second, while some dimensions of curriculum have commonly understood meanings, others do not. For example, most mathematics teachers would agree on what content falls within the categories of *square roots*, *quadratic equations*, and *slope*. But topics such as *math modeling* or *proportional reasoning* may be interpreted quite differently by different teachers. As we found in our analysis, the problem is particularly acute for curricular terms associated with the mathematics reform movement.

Third, coding a given teacher's artifacts requires many judgments, some of which may require inferences that go beyond the available data. Although textbooks need to be coded only for topic coverage, other artifacts have to be coded to extract information on topics, instructional characteristics of exams or assignments, level of understanding required of students, and teachers' instructional goals. Depending on the degree of aggregation desired, coding judgments can be made either across all artifacts of a given type (e.g., across all assignments); with each separate exam or assignment as the unit of analysis; or, at the most disaggregated level, on an item-by-item basis within a given assignment or exam.[7] Coding artifacts requires not only a

_____

[7]We chose a coding approach that falls somewhere in the middle of these three options. Topic coverage, level of understanding, and assignment characteristics were coded for assignments (homework, in-class exercises, quizzes) at the level of the individual assignment. However, coders were asked to make summary judgments about teachers' goals as they were evidenced across *all* their assignments (i.e., one judgment based on their approximately 20 assignments). For exams, the coding was done at a finer level of detail, with level of understanding coded for each individual item or question, and instructional goals coded for each exam. We paid closer attention to exams because, while both assignments and exams represent the enacted curriculum, we felt that exams communicate what teachers consider to be most important.

great number of judgments but also a variety of different kinds of judgments. In some cases, a textbook lesson, assignment, or exam item can be matched to one of the topics on the survey list. But other coding tasks require more complex judgments—e.g., identifying types of exam and assignment formats or making inferences about the purpose of an assignment or about a teacher's instructional goals. The number and variety of judgments involved in coding a teacher's artifacts provide considerable detail about the nature of his or her instruction and expand the number of benchmarks available to validate the survey results. However, the greater the number and variety of judgments coders have to make, the more difficult it is to ensure adequate reliability.

We attempted to optimize the validity and reliability of our coding by using six experienced secondary mathematics teachers as coders. The coders were trained by project staff for two days and were then supervised by two project staff who are also experienced mathematics teachers. During the two days, coders familiarized themselves with the coding manual and sample sets of artifacts. They also did practice coding, followed by extended discussions and refinement of the coding rules. The first artifact file took each coder about one day (approximately 7 hours) to complete, but the time required was reduced to about 2 to 4 hours per file once coders became more experienced.

Coders entered the information they extracted from the artifacts on a form that paralleled eight of the survey items (questions 11, 12, 13, 15, 16, 17, 21, and 23). Although the coders counted how often particular characteristics appeared in the artifacts, these continuous data were also transformed for some of the analyses into categorical data, with the categories matching the survey response scales. Each type of artifact required a somewhat different coding procedure. For textbooks, coders counted the number of lessons related to each of the topics on our survey. They were instructed to count only those lessons in which the topic formed an explicit focus of instruction and to exclude those in which the topic was included as prerequisite knowledge for the lesson. Coders also tallied topics for in-class assignments, homework, and quizzes, and in addition, they noted whether or not particular item types (e.g., multistep problems) were included. These item characteristics matched those listed on the survey. Exams were comparable to assignments, except that instead of recording only incidence, coders had to count how many exam items displayed each of the characteristics listed in the relevant survey questions.

About 15 percent (n = 11) of the artifact files were double-coded by project staff for reliability purposes. The rate of consistency between coders varied somewhat across the types of artifacts. For textbooks, coders had a rate of agreement of 58 percent on the exact number of lessons that included a particular topic; 74 percent of their judgments about topic inclusion differed by only one lesson; and 85 percent were within two lessons. On assignments, the coders had a rate of agreement of 74 percent on all their judgments about topic inclusion, instructional characteristics, and goals; they differed by only one category for 86 percent of the judgments they made; and they were within two categories on 91 percent. The rates for exams were 71, 78, and 81 percent, respectively, for the three levels of agreement.

Although these rates of agreement are reasonable, given the nature of the task, two caveats are in order. First, these aggregate rates mask the large number of judgments coders had to make. For example, for each assignment, coders were making 30 different judgments, a number that was then multiplied across the approximately 20 assignments each teacher provided. For exams, the number of separate judgments was 51, multiplied by the 5 or 6 exams from each teacher. A second caveat concerns what became an important factor in interpreting some of our substantive results: The aggregated rates mask considerable variation across types of judgments. On some items, the rates of agreement between coders were close to 100 percent, and in other instances, they fell below 50 percent. The items with the highest rates of agreement tended to be the more specific, narrower content topics (e.g., *complex numbers*) and traditional instructional approaches and goals (e.g., *proportion of exam items that are multiple choice, proportion that are minor variations of homework problems*). Those with the least agreement were either broad topic categories or more reform-oriented topics and approaches (e.g., *patterns and functions, problems having more than one possible answer*). Although our coders were experienced teachers, conversant with the NCTM standards and trained in a common set of decision rules, their lack of agreement evidenced some of the same confusion about terms that was reflected in teachers' responses. As a result, these coding problems helped inform our substantive findings and recommendations for improving future data collection.

In the next three chapters, we summarize major findings, focusing first on instructional content, then on instructional strategies, and finally, on instructional goals. In each chapter, we provide examples of the kinds of information about curriculum that can be obtained from teacher surveys. We then examine the level of consistency between survey responses and the artifacts, identify reasons for discrepancies, and suggest how these discrepancies might be reduced in future indicator efforts.

Chapter Three

INSTRUCTIONAL CONTENT

Instructional content—the topics covered in a particular course—forms the core of the implemented curriculum. Although it is mediated through the instructional strategies teachers use, content is the dimension of curriculum whose relationship to student achievement is the most well-established. It is also the aspect of curriculum that has proven the least problematic to measure through teacher surveys. National surveys such as NAEP and NELS have typically asked teachers whether they taught or reviewed any of the items on a general list of topics. By asking teachers whether their students had been taught the content reflected in specific test items, SIMS researchers expanded the type of survey questions used to probe topic coverage so that they could measure more precisely students' OTL. The SIMS experience, in particular, suggests that valid data on instructional content can be obtained from teacher surveys. Mean teacher OTL ratings provide a reasonably good predictor of between-system achievement differences and, consequently, have some predictive validity at the level of national education systems (Travers and Westbury, 1989).

However, despite the success of the SIMS strategy in documenting topic coverage, several questions remain about the reliability and validity of content data obtained from national surveys. First, most U.S. surveys ask about topics that are very general. Extant surveys either do not differentiate well the breadth or depth at which topics cutting across multiple courses are covered (e.g., polynomials, properties of geometric figures) or they do not probe deeper than the level of a course title (e.g, trigonometry, calculus) to measure specific course content. Second, surveys typically do not ask about the amount of time spent on a particular topic—i.e., the number of periods or lessons devoted to it. Finally, it is difficult to validate topic coverage in a cost-effective way for indicator purposes. Unless *all* of a teacher's exams and assignments are collected for an entire school year, these sources cannot provide an accurate picture of the topics covered or the depth of coverage. Textbooks are the obvious alternative because they typically span an entire course and can be collected and coded without burdening teachers. However, earlier research on elementary mathematics showed that teachers using the same text vary widely in their topic coverage and pacing (Freeman et al., 1983). Moreover, teachers do not typically cover an entire textbook and may supplement it with other materials; therefore, textbooks can be used as a source of validation only if information is also available about how they are used by individual teachers.

We tried to address each of these issues in designing our strategy for validating survey data about instructional content. As noted in the previous chapter, our survey contained topics at a greater level of specificity, in addition to the more general topics included on the NAEP and NELS surveys. Our survey also asked teachers about the number of periods devoted to each topic. Because of the need to validate topic coverage information that spanned an entire year, we relied on teachers' textbooks as the primary source for validation. However, we asked them exactly which chapters they covered and how closely they followed the textbook. Only those chapters that teachers indicated they had already covered or planned to cover by the end of the year were coded for content coverage. In addition, although we could not use either teachers' exams (because they covered only one semester) or their assignments and logs (which covered only five weeks) as a primary source for validating topic coverage, we did use them as a secondary source.

Our analysis suggests that the accuracy with which topic coverage is reported on teacher surveys differs across topics. Topics covered in upper-level courses tend to be reported with great accuracy, while those covered in lower-level courses, general topics, topics associated with the mathematics reform movement, and those that are used as tools in the learning and application of other topics (e.g., graphing, tables and charts) are reported less accurately. Before presenting the findings from our validation analysis, we provide some examples of the kinds of information that can be obtained from survey data on topic coverage.

ILLUSTRATIVE EXAMPLES

Topic coverage data is perhaps most useful for describing the distribution of students' opportunities to learn the content associated with a particular course. "Box and whiskers" plots illustrate how topic coverage in particular courses is distributed (see McDonnell et al., 1990; Kifer, 1993). We present similar data in this section, and then move beyond the standard of whether or not a set of topics has been taught as new content to showing the variation in the amount of class time spent on core topics.

Table 3.1 categorizes the topics from the survey that are commonly covered at four different course levels. These four sets of topics are not meant to be exhaustive, but they do represent at least part of the core content for each of the courses listed. Figure 3.1 compares the distribution of the pre-algebra and algebra topics taught as new content in courses below algebra I with those taught in algebra courses. Figure 3.2 makes the same comparisons but uses as a criterion whether the two sets of topics were taught for six or more periods, i.e., covered in some depth. The line across each box represents the median; the lower and upper boundaries of the box equal the 25th and 75th percentiles; the whiskers depict the 10th and 90th percentiles; and the dots represent outliers beyond the 10th and 90th percentiles.

Table 3.1

Representative Topics Covered at Four Course Levels

Pre-algebra and Arithmetic	Algebra I

Ratios, proportions, and percents
Conversions among fractions, decimals, and percents
Laws of exponents
Square roots
Applications of measurement formulas (e.g., area, volume)
	Polynomials
	   Linear equations
	   Slope
	   Writing equations for lines
	   Inequalities
	   Coordinate geometry
	   Distance, rate, time problems
	   Quadratic equations

Algebra II	Math analysis/Pre-calculus
Polynomials Quadratic equations Logarithms Conic sections Slope Sequences Matrices and matrix equations	Trigonometry Polar coordinates Complex numbers Vectors Limits

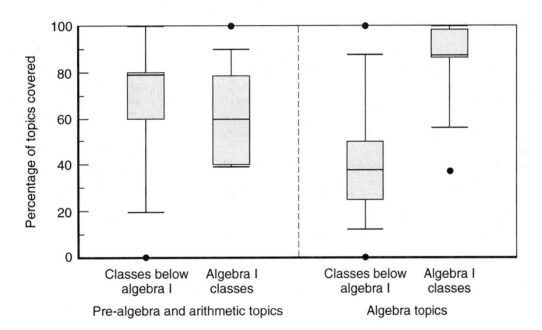

Figure 3.1—Proportion of Pre-Algebra and Algebra I Topics Taught as New Content, by Course Level

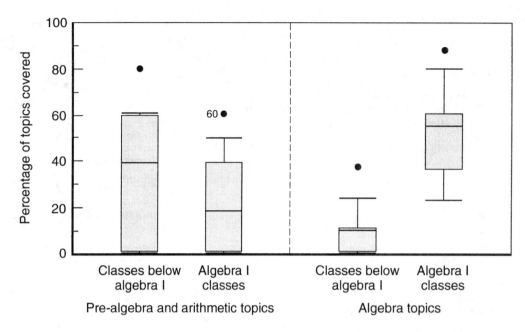

Figure 3.2—Proportion of Pre-Algebra and Algebra I Topics Taught as New Content for Six or More Class Periods, by Course Level

There is little variation in exposure to core algebra topics across the algebra I classes in our sample. Most classes cover 85 percent or more of the core topics. Yet a fair amount of attention in these classes is also paid to lower-level content, with the typical class also covering 60 percent of the pre-algebra and arithmetic topics as new content.

There is considerably greater variation in the proportion of algebra classes in which core topics are covered for longer periods of time (see Figure 3.2). In a typical class, about half of the topics are taught over six or more periods, but a few classes receive almost no in-depth coverage of algebra topics, while a few at the other end of the distribution spend extended time on most core topics. The plot showing the distribution of in-depth coverage of pre-algebra and arithmetic topics in the algebra classes indicates that while these classes may be covering a significant proportion of the lower-level topics, they are doing so for relatively brief periods of time. The typical algebra class covers only 20 percent of the pre-algebra topics for more than six periods.

In contrast to the algebra I classes, the pre-algebra classes in our sample show somewhat greater variation in topic coverage, but even at this level, most of the core topics are covered in the typical class (80 percent in the median class) (see Figure 3.1). The proportion of algebra I topics included in these classes varies considerably, with those in the top quartile getting some exposure to half or more of the algebra topics and those in the bottom quartile being exposed to about 20 percent or less of the algebra content. Figure 3.2 illustrates why asking about whether or not a topic was taught without asking about the amount of time spent on it can result in a misleading picture of OTL. As the plot showing the coverage of algebra I topics in pre-algebra classes indicates, the median class covers only 12 percent of the algebra topics for six or more periods. Just as the algebra teachers in our sample spent little time teaching lower-level content, the pre-algebra teachers introduced their students to algebra topics only briefly.

In contrast, there is little variation in coverage of the core course content in the algebra II and math analysis classes (see Figures 3.3 and 3.4). In the typical algebra II class, about 80 percent of the algebra II topics are covered, and about the same proportion of math analysis topics are covered in the math analysis courses. Nevertheless, in both courses, only about half of the core topics are covered for six or more periods. Still there is considerable overlap in topic coverage between the two courses, with the median algebra II class covering 40 percent of the math analysis topics (20 percent for six or more periods), and the median math analysis class covering 71 percent of the algebra II topics (35 percent for six or more periods).

This presentation of topic coverage illustrates how knowing the amount of class time spent on a set of topics provides a more accurate measure of students' OTL. With this additional information, we found that some students are receiving in-depth instruction on core topics, while others are introduced to them only briefly. Comparing topic coverage across course levels also allows us to estimate the distribution of course-level content that students are receiving, as compared with their exposure to topics that are either above or below the level of the course. This type of indicator data on topic coverage can provide a more thorough depiction of instructional con-

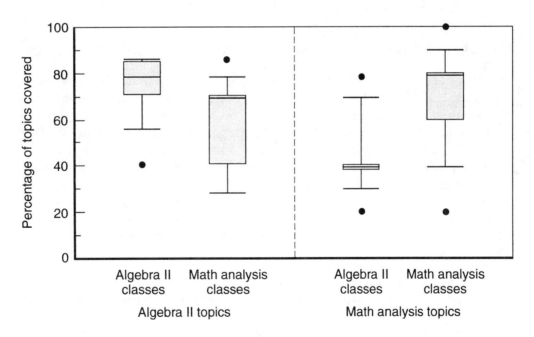

Figure 3.3—Proportion of Algebra II and Math Analysis Topics Taught as New Content, by Course Level

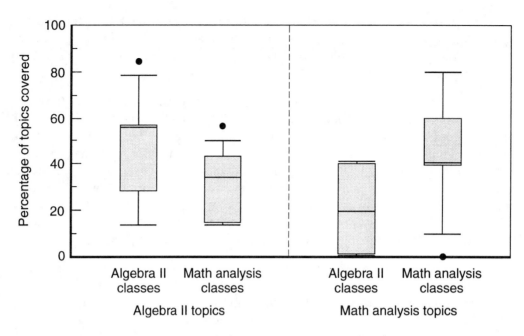

Figure 3.4—Proportion of Algebra II and Math Analysis Topics Taught as New Content for Six or More Class Periods, by Course Level

tent. However, the quality of that depiction depends on the accuracy of the survey data from which it is drawn.

CONSISTENCY BETWEEN THE SURVEYS AND THE COURSE TEXTBOOKS

For those chapters of their textbooks that teachers indicated they had covered or planned to cover before the end of the year, coders counted the number of lessons devoted to each of the topics listed on the post–artifact-data-collection survey.[1] These counts were then converted into the six response categories in question 11 of the survey,[2] using the algorithm outlined in the footnote to Table 3.2. The results are reported in terms of the proportion of cases in which coders' and teachers' estimates of the number of periods spent on a topic fell within the same response category on the survey (direct agreement) and the proportion of cases in which their respective estimates were within one response category as defined on the survey (e.g., if one's estimate was *1-2 periods* and the other's was *3-5 periods*, the agreement would be within one response category).

Across all topics, the average rate of direct agreement between the surveys and textbooks was 42 percent, and the rate within one survey response category was 72 per-

---

[1]The instructions to the coders defined a textbook lesson as a subsection of a chapter that typically consists of a two- to three-page "spread," with a page or two of explanation followed by a set of exercises. Coders were instructed to include all substantive subsections and to omit enrichment, computer, review, and chapter test sections.

[2]The six response categories were *0 periods, 1–2 periods, 3–5 periods, 6–10 periods, 11–20 periods,* and *>20 periods.*

cent. The average level of agreement suggests that although survey data may not provide a very precise picture of the time spent on different topics, such information is reasonably accurate for ascertaining that a topic has been taught not at all or for only a few periods, for a week or two, or for several weeks. Given that most OTL measures tend to be fairly crude (i.e., typically reporting whether or not a general topic has been covered, with no information about the time spent on it), being able to report topic coverage at this level of specificity represents a significant improvement.

But the mean rate of agreement masks significant differences across topics. Table 3.2 lists the topics (15 of the 40 included on the two forms of the survey) for which the

Table 3.2

Consistency Between Topic Coverage as Reported on Surveys and as Coded from Textbooks:[a]

Topics Where Direct Agreement Is <42 Percent and Agreement Within One Survey Response Category Is <72 Percent

Topic	Percent Direct Agreement	Percent Within One Category	Possible Explanation for Inconsistency
Linear equations	9	42	Low intercoder reliability (K = 0.259)
Conversion among fractions, decimals, percents	21	71	Use versus specific focus of teaching
Polynomials	22	55	Low intercoder reliability (K = 0.359)
Patterns and functions	23	65	Lack of understanding or common meaning among respondents
Conic sections	24	60	
Graphing	25	67	Use versus specific focus of teaching
Tables and charts	25	67	Use versus specific focus of teaching
Proportional reasoning	26	66	• Lack of understanding or common meaning among respondents • Low intercoder reliability (K = 0.067)
Ratios, proportion, percents	26	54	Low intercoder reliability (K = 0.189)
Inequalities	27	70	Low intercoder reliability (K = 0.324)
Slope	27	68	Low intercoder reliability (K = 0.324)
Mathematical modeling	28	51	Lack of understanding or common meaning among respondents
Sequences	30	59	
Estimation	33	71	Use versus specific focus of teaching
Matrices	42	70	

[a]Textbooks were coded for the number of lessons in which a topic was covered. Because textbooks divide material differently and include varying numbers of lessons, the number of textbook lessons covered by teachers ranged from 34 to 181, with a mean of 93.6 and a standard deviation of 29.8. In order to standardize across texts and to make valid comparisons with teachers' reports about the number of periods spent on a topic, the number of lessons on a given topic was divided by the total number of lessons and multiplied by 140, which is an approximation of the total number of periods of instruction in a given academic year. The resulting number was then converted into one of the six response options for reporting topic coverage on the survey (1 = *0 periods*; 2 = *1–2 periods*; 3 = *3–5 periods*; 4 = *6–10 periods*; 5 = *11–20 periods*; 6 = *>20 periods*).

rates of agreement were below the mean. Table 3.3 lists the eight topics for which the rates of agreement were highest. Five of these topics[3] are covered primarily in upper-level courses, so only a minority of the teachers in the sample reported spending any time on them. In addition, because the scope and sequence of upper-level courses tend to be more precisely defined (e.g., because of the requirements of AP tests and the narrower focus of the topics covered), teachers may be able to estimate more precisely the amount of time spent on a topic in these courses.

Table 3.3

Consistency Between Topic Coverage as Reported on Surveys and as Coded from Textbooks:[a]

Topics Where Direct Agreement Is >50 Percent and Agreement Within One Survey Response Category Is >80 Percent

Topic	Percent Direct Agreement	Percent Within One Category
Calculus	85	89
Measures of dispersion	81	92
Integration	81	96
Discrete mathematics	77	92
Growth and decay	67	87
Vectors	63	89
Probability	59	80
Statistics	51	82

[a]The process by which the textbook data were recoded to be comparable with the survey data on topic coverage is described in the footnote to Table 3.2.

Coding and Data Transformation Problems

We identified six possible reasons for the low rates of agreement. The first two stem from measurement problems associated with extracting topic coverage data from textbooks and converting those data into a form comparable to the estimates provided by teachers on the survey. First, although the double-coding of textbooks indicated that coder error had been kept to an acceptable level,[4] some topics were more prone to coder disagreement than others. Six of the 15 topics in Table 3.2 had only slight or fair rates of interrater agreement (i.e., a kappa statistic of <0.40),[5] and these were the lowest among the 40 topics coded. Although low intercoder reliability

---

[3]The five topics covered in upper-level courses are *calculus, measures of dispersion, integration, discrete mathematics,* and *vectors.*

[4]As noted in Chapter Two, on average, two coders agreed on the exact number of lessons devoted to a topic 58 percent of the time, were within one lesson 75 percent of the time, and were within two lessons 85 percent of the time.

[5]A kappa statistic is a measure of interrater agreement, adjusted for chance agreement, when there are two unique raters and two or more ratings It is scaled to be 0 when the amount of agreement is what would be expected to be observed by chance and 1 when there is perfect agreement. Moderate levels of agreement are conventionally interpreted as 0.41–0.60, substantial as 0.61–0.80, and almost perfect as 0.81–1.00. All but nine of the topics coded from the textbooks had moderate or higher levels of agreement, with 19 of the topics at or above the substantial level.

was found to be a problem for only a few topics, it does suggest that coders may need more training and ongoing monitoring than we provided.

The second reason relates to the algorithm we used in converting the continuous data on topic coverage, as reflected in the textbooks, into the same categories that teachers used on the surveys. We knew that textbook lessons may not be exactly comparable to periods of instruction as a unit of analysis, and that the number of days available for instruction varies by school and even for classes within the same school (e.g, depending on when assemblies, standardized testing, and the like are scheduled). Consequently, we tried to standardize the two measures of topic coverage in a variety of different ways (e.g., by raising or lowering the approximate number of periods of instruction over the year, and by examining only textbook lessons and topics reported on the survey as having already been covered), but none of these transformations produced significantly different rates of agreement.

Survey Design Issues

The next two reasons relate to survey design issues that we identified while framing the study. One is the high level of generality that characterizes the topics included on most national surveys. Because we assumed that specific topics will yield more valid data, as well as a more detailed picture of students' OTL, we included a greater number of specific topics on our post–data-collection survey. Several of those topics were elaborations of the NELS topics. As Table 3.4 indicates, the more specific topics had higher rates of agreement between the surveys and textbooks than did the general NELS topics. We recognize that there are tradeoffs associated with including longer topic lists, particularly on surveys that must serve multiple purposes. But our research suggests that, despite the potentially greater teacher burden, national surveys will need to be more comprehensive if they are to provide valid data on topic coverage.

Table 3.4

Rates of Agreement Between Surveys and Textbooks for General Topics and More Specific Elaborations

	Percent Direct Agreement[a]	Percent Within One Category
Linear equations	9	42
Slope	27	68
Writing equations for lines	53	74
Polynomials	22	55
Quadratic equations	43	70
Trigonometry	35	69
Polar coordinates	48	67
Statistics	51	82
Measures of dispersion	81	92

[a]Differences in the rate of agreement between each general topic and its more specific elaboration are significant at $p < 0.5$, with the exception of the "within one category" difference for trigonometry and polar coordinates.

Another factor likely to affect the reliability and validity of survey data on topic coverage is the time frame over which teachers are asked both to recall what they have already taught and to estimate what they will teach over the rest of the year. We assumed that such data are likely to be considerably less precise than data on topic coverage reported concurrently with the actual teaching. We were able to test that assumption by comparing teachers' reports of topic coverage on their daily logs with the assignments they made over the same five weeks. Eleven topics were reported as being covered over this period by at least one-third of the teachers. Across those topics, the rate of direct agreement was 58 percent, and the rate within one category was 83 percent, using the same response categories as the survey. To ensure that this higher rate of agreement was not an artifact of converting the continuous data from the logs and assignments into the survey categories, we also calculated the rate of agreement between the exact number of periods teachers reported covering a topic and the number of times coders identified it as being included on the assignments. We found that the average rate of agreement within one class period or assignment was 40 percent, and the rate within two was 59 percent. The improvement in the quality of data collected simultaneously with the teaching of a topic is illustrated by the fact that eight of the eleven topics are also those that had the lowest rates of agreement between the survey and the text. Using the log and assignment data multiplied the rate of agreement by between 1.5 and 2.5 times for these topics.

Clearly, asking teachers to report on their topic coverage concurrently with their teaching of the content is not a feasible strategy for routine data collection in national surveys. The gains in improved reliability would be offset by an incomplete picture of the content presented to students throughout the year. In addition, having a large number of teachers report on a daily basis for even several weeks might increase the costs of national surveys and would most likely result in a lower overall response rate.

Sources of Inconsistency Identified in the Analysis

The final two reasons represent substantive findings from our analysis of the survey and artifact data. One explanation emerged from our follow-up interviews with a subsample of the teachers, conducted because we noted internal inconsistencies in their surveys (most notably between reports about instructional goals and those about activities) that suggested there was a lack of common understanding of some terms associated with the mathematics reform movement. We asked teachers how they defined the topics that showed the most inconsistency and found that three appeared to present special problems for respondents. One of these—*proportional reasoning*—was also the one with the lowest level of interrater agreement. Teachers told us that the term *proportional reasoning* was vague; some reported that they had never seen the two words combined. Several teachers participating in the group interviews volunteered that they had no idea what the term *math modeling* meant, even though it appears in key mathematics reform documents (National Research Council, 1989; California Department of Education, 1992). Interviewees argued that the two concepts *patterns* and *functions* should be separated because they are not parallel or necessarily linked. The newer reform literature (California Department of Education, 1992) seems to agree with our teacher respondents on this issue and argues against NCTM's (1989) joining the two concepts. The rationale is that patterns are broadly applicable in many or perhaps all strands of mathematics, while functions comprise one specific way of generalizing an observed pattern. Although the problem of teachers either not understanding the meaning of a term or interpreting it differently is considerably greater for instructional activities and goals than for topics, these examples do suggest that some survey data cannot be validly interpreted during a time in which language and accompanying practice are in transition. While only a few topics may fall in this category, they are the ones of potentially greatest interest for charting trends in curricular reform.

Finally, we found that teachers reported spending greater amounts of time on teaching four of the topics with low rates of agreement than the coders estimated. These four topics—*conversion among fractions, decimals, and percents; graphing; tables and charts*; and *estimation*—are all tools or building blocks that students can draw upon in working problems on other substantive topics. For example, some geometry textbooks have students record their measurements of geometric figures in a table format. Although *tables and charts* is not the specific focus of teaching during such exercises, the topic is being used by students. We believe that teachers' overestimation of their coverage of these four topics stems from their not making a distinction between having students use the concept while working on other topics and having the topic as the primary focus of a substantive lesson. This problem can be addressed by including clearer instructions in survey prompts.[6]

CONCLUSIONS

Our analysis suggests that teacher survey data can provide a reasonably accurate picture of topic coverage. If the standard is knowing whether or not a topic has been taught and, if it has been taught, whether it has been covered over several periods, for a week or two, or for several weeks, then teacher self-reports are reliable. However, our data provide a strong rationale for including more specific curricular topics on surveys. Not only do they provide a more detailed and comprehensive picture of students' OTL, but teachers' reports on these topics are more reliable than their reports about general topics which encompass multiple subtopics and for which it is difficult to make precise time estimates. We recognize the tradeoffs in requesting more detailed information about topic coverage, but we would argue that the topics currently included on national surveys such as NELS provide data that are too general to be useful, particularly for measuring OTL. Consequently, the gains in both reliability and validity may more than offset the additional burden.

---

[6]As indicated in Table 3.2, we found that three reasons helped explain most of the lowest rates of agreement between the textbooks and the surveys. However, for three topics—*conic sections, sequences,* and *matrices*—none of these reasons apply. The rate of interrater agreement was moderate or above for these topics, teacher respondents agreed on their meaning, and teachers did not systematically overestimate their coverage of these topics as they did for topics that might be classified as tools.

Our artifact analysis suggests that in addition to the need for more detailed, enhanced topic lists on national surveys, validation studies are necessary to pinpoint the sources of measurement problems. One area that will continue to be problematic is the lack of common agreement on the meaning of key terms associated with the mathematics reform movement. Such terms need to be included on national surveys to chart trends in topic coverage; but without accompanying validation studies, the data are likely to be misinterpreted. Consequently, the use of in-depth interviews and focus groups to supplement artifact analyses will help to identify the different understandings that teachers hold of concepts central to expected changes in mathematics teaching. But even without the current flux in curricular practices, validation studies would still be necessary. By collecting detailed data from multiple sources over shorter periods of time (e.g., through daily logs and assignments), validation studies can provide a benchmark against which to judge the reliability of routine survey data that require teachers to recall and estimate topic coverage over longer periods of time.

Chapter Four

INSTRUCTIONAL STRATEGY

Instructional strategy is a multifaceted dimension of curriculum that is considerably more difficult to measure than instructional content. This concept embodies all the approaches used in the teaching and learning process. It includes what teachers do (e.g., lecture, lead discussions, work with small groups) and what students do (e.g., work individually or in groups, work on projects, use manipulatives). But it also includes the type of work students are assigned, the focus and format of that work, how it is evaluated, and the level of understanding expected of students.

In addition to the problems caused by its scope, instructional strategy is also difficult to measure because surveys typically cannot capture the subtle differences in how teachers define and use different techniques. For example, one teacher might lecture directly from the textbook and do most of the talking in the class. Another might draw on material from sources other than the textbook and engage students in lively give-and-take exchanges. Without a detailed set of survey probes, however, both teachers are likely to report that they spend most of the period lecturing. Even a detailed survey would probably fall short in representing the two classrooms because it could not adequately measure the nature of the interactions between students and teachers,[1] yet someone observing the classrooms would identify two very different kinds of instruction.

Despite these major limitations, there is still much that survey data can tell us about instructional strategy. Survey data can describe the major dimensions of classroom processes and how they vary across course levels and types of schools. National survey data, collected periodically, can document trends in teachers' use of generic instructional strategies. Such information is important for determining whether or not teaching is changing in ways consistent with the expectations of curriculum reformers and policymakers.

ILLUSTRATIVE EXAMPLES

The clearest picture of instruction that emerges from our survey data is that teachers rely on a few strategies that they use frequently. A large proportion of teachers re-

---

[1]This shortcoming of survey instrumentation also applies to artifact data. In fact, artifact data are particularly weak in their ability to portray instructional strategies that do not involve written work of some kind.

ported engaging in traditional activities such as lecturing (87 percent) and correcting or reviewing homework (86 percent) on a daily basis, and the majority reported engaging in activities consistent with the mathematics reform movement only infrequently or not at all—e.g., 65 percent of the teachers reported having student-led discussions once or twice a semester or not at all; 61 percent rarely or never discussed career opportunities in mathematics; and only 49 percent have their students work in small groups at least once or twice a week.[2]

Calculator use in these classrooms is very high, with 74 percent of the teachers reporting that students use them almost daily. Usage is just the opposite for computers, however. Students use computers on a daily basis in less than 2 percent of the courses, and in over half of the classes (52 percent), computers are never used to solve exercises or problems.[3] Most teachers reported that the majority of class time is spent in direct instruction; student discipline and administrative tasks such as taking attendance consume less than 10 percent of teachers' in-class time.

The tendency in national indicator reports such as those produced by NAEP (e.g., Mullis et al., 1991; 1994) has been to focus on single questionnaire items, examining each teaching strategy separately rather than seeking to understand how teachers link discrete strategies to create instructional repertoires. Given that teachers rarely use just one strategy and typically rely on several even in the same lesson, reporting on an item-by-item basis fails to produce a coherent picture of instruction. We examined our survey data in several ways to see if they could enable us to identify different instructional repertoires in which teachers combine a number of separate strategies. Our first approach consisted of grouping instructional techniques according to the strategies advocated in reform documents such as the NCTM Professional Standards (1991) and the California mathematics framework (1992). We also created a list of techniques that seemed to represent the traditional teaching repertoire to which the reform documents were reacting. Table 4.1 shows the two groups of strategies. To test the consistency of these groupings, we scaled them and found that they cohered reasonably well with an alpha of 0.72 for the reform scale and 0.62 for the traditional scale. The parts of the scale that were intended to operate in a negative direction (e.g., not lecturing as part of the reform repertoire) did in fact reverse as expected.

We also conducted a factor analysis to identify instructional strategies that occur together. Three factors emerged that seem to have substantive meaning. The first, shown in Table 4.2, is dominated by discussion strategies that strongly emphasize the role of students in class discussions. The second has a clear demonstration component; student participation strategies are part of this repertoire, but it is much more teacher-directed than the first one. The third factor, with only two compo-

---

[2]The lack of variation in teachers' instructional strategies that we found in our sample is consistent with findings from other studies based on a variety of data, including classroom observations (for example, see Goodlad, 1984; Oakes, 1985; Gamoran and Nystrand, 1991).

[3]The low incidence of computer use reported in our sample is similar to the level found by Weiss (1994) in her national survey of high school science and mathematics teachers, 56 percent of whose classes never use computers. The level of teacher lecture, textbook usage, and small-group work in our sample is also similar to the patterns documented by Weiss.

Table 4.1

Instructional Repertoire Scales

	Reform	Traditional
Whole class discusses small groups' solutions	+	
Small groups work on problems	+	
Student-led discussions	+	
Students give oral reports	+	
Students work on problems with no obvious method of solution	+	
Students use computers	+	
Students work on projects in class	+	
Students respond to questions that require writing at least a paragraph	+	−
Students use tables and graphs	+	−
Students work with manipulatives	+	−
Administer a test	−	
Lecture	−	+
Teacher demonstrates an exercise at board	−	+
Students respond orally to questions		+
Teacher-led discussions		+
Review homework		+
Students read textbooks		+
Teacher summarizes lesson's main points		+
Students work on next day's homework		+
Students practice computational skills		+
Students use calculators		−
Scale reliability (Cronbach's alpha):	0.72	0.62

nents, is the closest to what would be considered traditional teaching, with the teacher lecturing and students responding to the teacher's questions.[4]

The lack of variation in classroom practice across the teachers in our sample is the primary reason that most of the instructional strategies included on our survey do not fit into a common factor space. Nevertheless, the coherence of the reform and traditional-practice scales and the high face validity of the factors that did emerge suggest that future efforts to link instructional strategies and student outcomes

---

[4]In a further attempt to gauge how well these factors fit the data, we also performed a confirmatory factor analysis using structural equation modeling procedures on the subset of 12 variables that load most strongly on the three factors. This analysis indicated that the three factors do not satisfactorily model all of the observed variation, though the resulting "goodness of fit" indices were close enough to acceptable levels that the notion of instructional repertoires is still plausible. (For a well-fitting model, the fit indices should be >0.90. Ours were as follows: Bentler and Bonnett's nonnormed index = 0.80, normed fit index = 0.68, Bollen's nonnormed index delta = 0.86.)

The analysis did show places where the survey needs improvement. For example, the variables *teacher uses manipulatives* and *students use manipulatives* proved to have highly correlated error terms, indicating nonsubstantive sources of covariation, such as their wording or placement on the survey.

Table 4.2

Instructional Repertoire Factor Matrix[a]

	Factor 1	Factor 2	Factor 3
Whole class discusses small groups' solutions	0.74	−0.03	0.21
Small groups work on problems	0.71	0.01	0.00
Teacher-led discussions	0.70	−0.00	0.37
Student-led discussions	0.67	−0.13	0.02
Students use calculators	0.55	0.01	−0.10
Students work individually	−0.54	−0.06	0.09
Administer a test	0.17	−0.70	−0.08
Students work with manipulatives	0.21	0.58	0.00
Teacher demonstrates an exercise at board	−0.34	0.56	0.29
Teacher uses manipulatives to demonstrate a concept	0.35	0.55	0.05
Students respond orally to questions	0.23	−0.14	0.87
Lecture	−0.09	−0.14	0.77
Students respond to questions that require writing at least a paragraph	0.46	0.41	−0.25
Students work on next day's homework	−0.45	−0.12	0.40
Students work on problems with no obvious method of solution	0.43	0.17	0.12
Students use tables and graphs	0.41	0.37	0.37
Students practice computation skills	−0.35	−0.34	0.02
Students work on exercises at board	0.20	0.47	0.20
Students give oral reports	0.19	0.17	−0.05
Teacher summarizes lesson's main points	−0.17	0.56	0.52
Students work on projects in class	0.09	0.41	−0.12
Students read textbooks	0.08	0.24	0.27
Discuss career opportunities	0.06	−0.12	0.50
Review homework	−0.02	0.08	0.15
Administer a quiz	−0.02	0.34	−0.20
Students use computers	0.00	0.29	−0.13
Eigenvalue	4.62	2.93	2.14

[a]Our exploratory analysis extracted six factors, three of which were substantively interpretable. The coefficients are from a promax rotation of the solution.

should move away from separate analyses of single questionnaire items and focus greater attention on identifying and understanding instructional repertoires. Although the clusters of instructional activities illustrated by our data are only suggestive, and additional research is needed on the conceptualization and measurement of such repertoires, they do argue for a different kind of reporting on national indicator data than has been done traditionally.

The picture of instruction that emerges from our survey data is quite consistent across course levels. As might be expected, teachers of algebra I and courses below that level had students practice or drill on computational methods more frequently than teachers of higher-level courses. In addition, the number of minutes per day of homework that teachers assigned was significantly greater for higher-level courses, with the mean ranging from only 19 minutes per day in courses below algebra I to 32 minutes a day for algebra I and 55 minutes a day for calculus. However, there were few other significant differences across course levels. Teachers in higher-level courses were just as likely as those in lower-level courses to lecture frequently, have students work on their next day's homework in class, and then correct or review that homework. Similarly, the infrequency of strategies such as student-led discussions and small-group work was quite similar across course levels.

One course, however, does seem to rely on different teaching strategies. Although the number of calculus classes in our sample was too small to permit any generalizations, those classes differed from the other courses in the sample in several major ways. In particular, calculus teachers reported lecturing less frequently and relying more on small-group work by students. But with this exception, the similarities across courses in our sample are far more striking than the differences.

CONSISTENCY BETWEEN THE SURVEYS AND THE ARTIFACTS

Since instructional strategy is the dimension of curriculum least amenable to validation through written artifacts, we were limited in our ability to measure the consistency of survey responses with other data. However, for 14 of the 26 instructional practice items on the surveys, we could compare teachers' survey responses at the end of the semester with their daily log entries during the five weeks of artifact data collection. We were also able to compare teachers' survey responses about the format and other characteristics of their exams and quizzes with their artifacts. Finally, we were able to compare teachers' actual homework assignments with their responses to a survey question about the characteristics of those assignments.

Logs and Surveys

Table 4.3 shows the rate of exact agreement between the surveys and the logs on the frequency with which teachers reported engaging in a variety of instructional activities. The level of agreement within one survey response category is also reported.[5] Given that the data in this table compare information that teachers provided at three intervals over the course of the semester (the last time within one week of completing

---

[5]To compare the survey responses with the log entries, we had to convert the continuous data from the logs—i.e., how many times over the 25 days of data collection teachers reported engaging in an activity—into the categorical response options used in question 13 on the survey. Anything that was done 60 percent or more of the time (>15 days) was recoded as *almost every day*; any activity that occurred 25–59 percent of the time (5–14 days) was recoded as *once or twice a week*; and activities that occurred 24 percent of the time or less (<5 times) were recoded as *once or twice a month*. We included *never* as a comparison category, but we did not have a comparison category for *once or twice a semester* for the log data.

Table 4.3

**Consistency Between the Reported Frequency of Instructional Activities on the Logs
and the Surveys**

	Percent Direct Agreement	Percent Within One Survey Response Category
Administer a test	60	83
Have students work exercises at the board	59	92
Lecture	57	97
Use manipulatives to demonstrate a concept	53	84
Have students work with other students in small groups	50	100
Demonstrate exercise at the board	50	85
Have students work on a computer	49	87
Have students work with manipulatives	48	87
Have students use a calculator	47	91
Have students work individually on written assignments	43	83
Correct or review homework in class	38	85
Have students work on next day's homework in class	35	62
Have teacher-led whole group discussions	35	87
Mean rate of agreement	48	87

the survey), with their responses to the survey completed at the end of the semester, the rate of direct agreement is quite low.[6]

The relatively high rate of agreement within one survey response category does suggest, however, that the problem may lie in how the survey response categories were constructed. The distinctions among them may not have been sufficiently discrete or meaningful to respondents. To check this possibility, we compared the mean frequency of instructional activities, as reported on the logs, with the category teachers used in responding to the survey. We found that the response options teachers used on the surveys did not always reflect actual differences in the frequencies of instructional activities as they were reported on the logs. The most common problem was the lack of significant differences in the frequency of activities as reported on the logs for the survey response categories *almost every day* and *once or twice a week*, and for *once or twice a week* and *once or twice a month*. For 8 of the 14 activities for which a comparison was made, the mean for two of the survey categories was virtually the

[6]In comparing the survey and log data, we chose to use the rate of direct agreement and the rate of agreement within one survey response category as our measures of consistency. Porter et al. (1993) made similar comparisons between log and survey data, using correlation coefficients as the measure of consistency. That study found the correlations between log and questionnaire data to be "substantial," (2-31) and concluded that "the validation results were very encouraging" (A-5).

Although the correlations for 7 of the 14 instructional practice items on our survey and log were greater than 0.50 (and significant at the 0.01 level), and only two items had correlations below 0.30 (with one significant at the 0.05 level and the other nonsignificant), we did not find this analysis to be very informative. Correlation coefficients conflate matches and mismatches across categories in a way that makes it difficult to retrieve information about specific patterns of responses to the two types of data collection instruments. A clearer and more intuitively attractive way to compare the two is to examine the closeness of agreement between the two indicators. The percentage agreement statistic measures that level of consistency directly.

same.[7] Although respondents reported no problems in using these response categories, the log data suggest that teachers who had engaged in an activity with the same frequency used different categories in reporting on it on their surveys. The response categories that are the most problematic are *almost every day* and *once or twice a week*, with the log data suggesting that reliable distinctions cannot be made between these two categories, based on survey data.

Exams and Surveys

Another aspect of instructional strategy that we were able to validate from the artifacts was the format and characteristics of teachers' exams. Teachers were asked to indicate the proportion of their tests and quizzes that were *multiple choice, short answer, essay*, and *open-ended problems*. In addition, they were asked to indicate the proportion of their exams that included items with certain characteristics such as requiring students to describe how to solve problems or problems with more than one possible answer or approach. Figures 4.1, 4.2, and 4.3 compare the means for the survey responses and the artifact coding.

On 6 of the 15 questions teachers were asked about their exams, the level of agreement between teachers and coders was 90 percent or higher. There was high agreement between teachers and coders on the proportion of exam items that were multiple choice (with the difference in means between the two sources less than 3

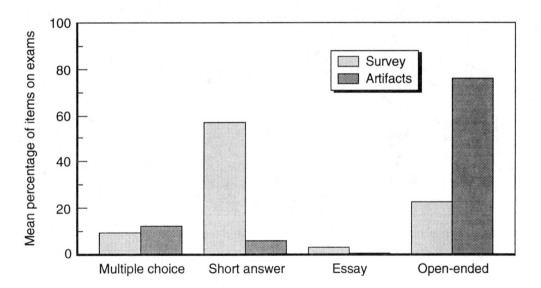

Figure 4.1—Comparison of Item Formats on Exams

---

[7]For example, for *lecture*, the mean over the 25 days of data collection for teachers indicating *almost every day* on their survey was 14.8, and for those reporting *once or twice a week*, 12.6. For *teacher-led discussion*, the means were 12.8 and 12.1, respectively; for *demonstrate an exercise at the board*, 15.4 and 14. Similarly, for *administer a test*, the mean for *once or twice a week* was 4.2, and for *once or twice a month*, 4.3.

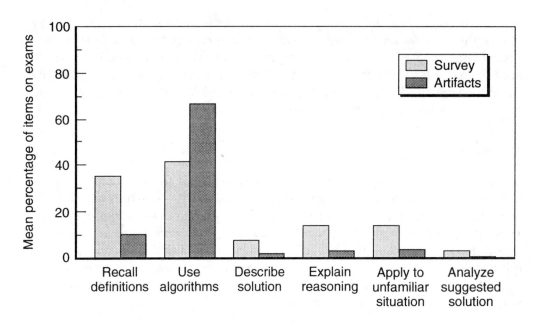

Figure 4.2—Comparison of Exam Item Characteristics

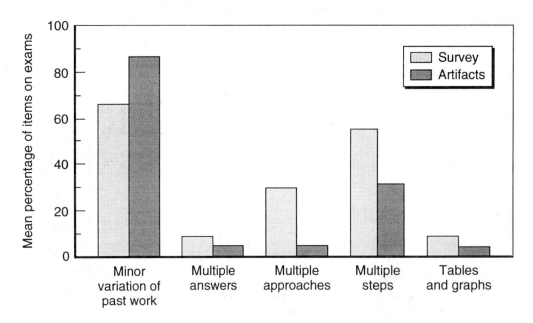

Figure 4.3—Comparison of Exam Problem Types

percent) and the proportion that were essay (the difference in means was 3 percent). Similarly, there was high agreement on the proportion of test items requiring the use of tabular or graphical data, the proportion requiring students to describe how to solve problems, and the proportion of problems with more than one answer. However, there were major disagreements between survey respondents and coders about the proportion of exam items that were short answer (a difference of about 50 percent between the two sources) and the proportion that were open-ended problems (a 51 percent difference).

Other questions where the level of disagreement between the surveys and the artifacts was greater than 20 percent were the proportion of exam items requiring students to recognize or recall definitions; the proportion requiring the use of algorithms to solve problems; the proportion that are minor variations of homework, class exercises, or problems; the proportion with more than one possible approach; and the proportion requiring more than one step to reach a solution. As illustrated in Figures 4.1 through 4.3, the coding of teachers' exams presents a more traditional picture of their approach to evaluating students than they reported on their surveys. According to the artifacts, teachers were less likely to include items that required students to describe how they solved problems, explain their reasoning, or apply concepts to different or unfamiliar situations than they indicated on their surveys. Similarly, the exams evidenced a smaller proportion of items with more than one possible answer or approach or that required more than one step to reach a solution than respondents estimated on their surveys.

The most problematic survey response categories concerning exam characteristics were *short answer, open-ended problems,* and the difference between the two. Even though the survey instrument defined open-ended problems as those *where students generate their own solutions,* teacher respondents and coders viewed the exam formats quite differently, with teachers tending to classify as short answer those items that coders categorized as open-ended problems. In classifying exam items, coders used a narrow definition for short answer—viz., a question requiring students to complete a sentence or fill in the blanks. However, our follow-up interviews indicated that while some teachers had interpreted the term more broadly, they also differed in their definitions. For example:

> *Math B teacher:* Short answer is giving students a specific question to answer. On the other [open-ended problems], students can go in different directions and they are graded on how in-depth their answer is.

> *Calculus teacher:* A short answer is when students are following standard procedures. I use open-ended when I'm introducing new topics and I don't give students a way to do it. I give them a good background on what they should be finding, but I don't guide them. An open-ended problem . . . is more about what students are expected to do, than the format of the test. Just because a test doesn't have a blank to fill in for the answer doesn't make it open-ended.

> *Intermediate math teacher:* What's the difference among short answer, essay, and open-ended? They're all the same.

The differing interpretations of these seemingly straightforward terms, as evidenced in the discrepancies between the survey responses and the exam coding and in the follow-up interviews, illustrate the need to define a number of survey items more precisely. A more precise set of response options for questions about exam format might be:

- Multiple choice

- Problems where students generate a solution and show their work, but no written explanation is required

- Problems where students generate a solution, show their work, *and* are also expected to explain their work in writing

This set eliminates the ambiguity inherent in distinguishing among short answer, essay, and open-ended items, while making a clear distinction between multiple choice and constructed responses and, within the constructed-response category, between answers that require written explanation in addition to mathematical calculations and those that do not.

Homework Assignments and Surveys

Teachers' daily homework assignments are a final source of validation about their instructional strategies. Teachers were asked on the survey how often they assigned certain types of homework, and their actual homework assignments were then coded to determine the extent to which they reflected the responses about these characteristics. For assignments that were not done entirely during class time, the rate of direct agreement between the survey responses and the artifact coding was 48 percent, and the agreement within one response category was 73 percent.[8] Behind this overall level of agreement is the same pattern that appeared for other types of instructional strategies. The teachers in our sample rely on only a few types of assignments, and while they report the predominance of these in their survey responses, they still indicate greater variety in their assignments than was identified in the artifacts. Ninety-one percent of the assignments in our artifact file were either exercises or problems from the textbook (72 percent) or exercises or problems from worksheets (19 percent). Similarly, 83 percent of the teachers reported on their surveys that they assign textbook problems at least once or twice a week, and 72 percent report assigning worksheet problems with the same frequency. A substantial proportion of teachers also reported that they *never* give homework assignments that require students to write definitions of concepts (40 percent), solve problems for which there is no obvious method of solution (23 percent), or extend results established in class (29 percent). Another sizable group of teachers reported using these more innovative homework strategies and going beyond textbook problems—e.g., over half reported assigning homework problems with no obvious method of solution at least once or twice a month. However, the artifacts show more traditional homework assignments, with considerably less variety in the type of tasks required of students.

---

[8]Of the 1,407 individual assignments in our artifact sample, 230 (16 percent) were worked on only during class, 389 (28 percent) were worked on by students both during and outside class, and 223 (16 percent) were done only outside class; for the remaining 563 (40 percent), teachers did not designate where the assignments were done. In comparing artifacts with the responses to question 21, we chose to include all assignments except those that were done only during class time, because we assumed most of the undesignated ones were homework assignments. However, we also checked the rate of agreement between the survey and those assignments that were done either completely outside class or worked on both during and outside of class. The rate of direct agreement was 42 percent, and the agreement within one response category was 69 percent—essentially the same pattern as for the larger set of assignments.

The artifacts indicate that the proportion of teachers who never use innovative homework strategies exceeds the survey reports by a factor of 2 to 4, depending on the strategy. Not surprisingly, the rate of agreement between the two data sources is lowest for the more innovative homework strategies.[9]

CONCLUSIONS

To the extent that we were able to validate the survey data on teachers' instructional strategies, we found that those data report accurately the instructional strategies used most often by teachers, and they provide some indication of how teachers combine strategies during instruction. Although the picture of teaching that can be drawn from survey data is not fine-grained, it is likely to be valid because both the survey and the artifact data clearly show that there is little variation in teachers' instructional strategies. Basically, the majority of teachers use a few instructional strategies and use them often.

Survey data are, however, limited in the precision with which they can measure how frequently teachers use particular strategies. Although teachers may find it easier to respond to questions that provide the five response categories typically included on national surveys, valid distinctions can probably be made only among activities that are done weekly or more often, monthly, once or twice a semester (i.e., infrequently), and never. Our analysis suggests that the distinction between daily activities and those done once or twice a week is not reliable.

Our comparison of teachers' reports on their exam formats, as compared with an analysis of their actual exams, provides an example of an area where a rather simple rewording of survey response options could produce more meaningful data. But the other inconsistencies we identified are symptomatic of a more serious problem. Teachers see their exams and assignments as exhibiting greater variety in their underlying instructional strategies than was evidenced in the artifact coding. Part of the problem might be addressed by providing more precise definitions of what is meant, for example, by *problems with more than one possible approach* or *problems that require more than one step to reach a solution*. However, discrepancies between the two types of data sources suggest more serious problems. Teachers see their instruction as more varied and less traditional than is reflected in their exams and assignments, and they do not share common meanings for some of the terms used by curriculum reformers.

The implications for the design of more reliable and valid survey instruments are unclear at this point because so few teachers have adopted the instructional strategies advocated by NCTM and similar groups. Consequently, it is difficult even to conduct valid pilot studies of alternative wordings of survey questions or to test new measures of instructional strategies. In the next chapter, we attempt to identify more

---

[9]Assignment characteristics for which the direct rate of agreement between the two data sources was 30 percent or lower included *reading the text or supplementary materials* (30 percent), *applying concepts or principles to different or unfamiliar situations* (13 percent), *solving problems for which there is no obvious method of solution* (30 percent), and *solving applied problems* (28 percent).

precisely the sources of problems and to suggest some possible solutions for measuring curriculum during a time of transition. We do so by examining teachers' reports on their instructional goals and comparing those reports with the goals reflected in their artifacts and with our analysis of their instructional strategies.

Chapter Five

INSTRUCTIONAL GOALS

The final dimension of curriculum consists of the goals or objectives teachers pursue as they present course content, using different instructional strategies. Arguments for including measures of teachers' instructional goals as indicators of curriculum rest on the assumption that the relative emphasis teachers accord different goals reveals something about their choices of instructional strategies. Furthermore, some empirical evidence suggests that teachers using the same textbook emphasize different aspects of it because they value the purposes of instruction differently (for a discussion of reasons for including goals as curriculum indicators, see Oakes and Carey, 1989).

However, teachers' reports of their course objectives reflect *intended* behavior and are less likely to be reliable than reports of *actual* behavior, such as topic coverage and instructional activities. Despite the obvious problems associated with measuring instructional goals, it has been argued that questions about teachers' goals should be included in national surveys because they serve as lead indicators showing the direction in which coursework and teaching in a particular subject may be heading. For example, teachers may report giving some emphasis to goals associated with the mathematics reform movement as a precursor to their engaging in activities consistent with those goals. While, in some instances, teachers' goals may signal a future change in their behavior, evidence from the implementation of educational innovations suggests that it would be inappropriate to make such an inference in reporting national trends. As McLaughlin (1990) notes in her overview of findings from implementation research, teachers' beliefs may sometimes follow rather than lead their changes in practice, especially if the changes in practice are mandated. For example, teachers may be required to integrate topics across different subject areas or have students write in journals, but their belief in the value of those practices may come only after they see that the changes have positive effects on their students.

Our research confirms the fact that instructional goals are the most problematic dimension of curriculum to measure. The consistency between survey responses on goals and instructional artifacts was the lowest among the three dimensions we studied. However, in examining the reasons for the inconsistency, we did learn something about teachers' perceptions and how they integrate new expectations and strategies into their current approach to teaching. Consequently, we first describe how the teachers in our sample viewed their goals and how the emphasis they reported giving these goals related to their reported use of instructional strategies. We then examine the consistency of teachers' self-reports with what coders found reflected in teachers' exams and assignments.

ILLUSTRATIVE EXAMPLES

Teachers were asked to rate the emphasis they gave to 20 different instructional goals. Although emphasis on traditional goals was greater, a majority of the respondents also reported emphasizing the reform goals. At least half of the teachers reported placing a moderate or major emphasis on analyzing different approaches, applying models to the real world, and using tables and graphs (see Figure 5.1).[1] A majority of the teachers also emphasized traditional goals such as solving and writing equations, memorizing facts, and performing calculations (Figure 5.2).

As we did with instructional activities, we grouped the instructional goals associated with the mathematics reform movement into one set and those that could be considered more traditional into another set. The scales are shown in Table 5.1. The reform goals scaled well, but the traditional goals did not. We can only speculate that the conventional goals did not scale well because they are not based on a coherent theory of instruction. Rather, they represent individual goals that teachers have traditionally pursued, perhaps without regard to the linkages among them.

We also conducted a factor analysis to determine if some subsets of goals were related to each other in a meaningful way. Four factors emerged that could be substantively interpreted (see Table 5.2). The first factor in Table 5.2 includes six items that deal with students developing critical thinking skills. The second factor includes five items that stress having students understand mathematical relationships in different ways and place little emphasis on memorization. Like the first two factors, the third is consistent with the goals of the mathematics reform movement and deals with the application of mathematics to other subjects and to daily life. The fourth factor represents a combined goal that has been stressed in a number of state curricular reforms, including Kentucky's—an emphasis on open-ended problem-solving and written explanation and a deemphasis on generating solutions to routine equations.[2]

---

[1]A majority of respondents reported placing a moderate or major emphasis on *learning to represent problem structures in multiple ways* (79 percent), *integrating different branches of mathematics* (76 percent), *raising questions and formulating conjectures* (77 percent), *finding examples and counterexamples* (66 percent), *judging the validity of arguments* (51 percent), and *discovering generalizations* (69 percent), in addition to the three reform goals shown in Figure 5.1.

[2]As we did for our investigation of instructional repertoires, we also performed a confirmatory factor analysis on a subset of 18 high-loading variables. This analysis indicated that the four factors modeled the observed measures reasonably well, since most of the fit indices were in an acceptable range (Bentler and Bonnett's nonnormed index = 0.89, normed fit index = 0.60, Bollen's nonnormed index delta = 0.91).

The four factors proved to be somewhat correlated, and there were also three pairs of goals with correlated error terms: *designing a project* and *writing at least a paragraph, raising questions* and *increasing interest in math*, and *raising questions and discovering generalizations*.

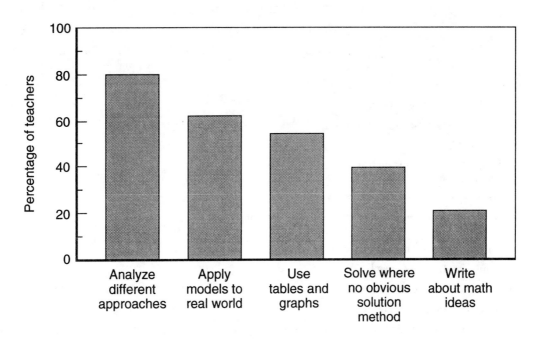

**Figure 5.1—Proportion of Teachers Reporting Major or Moderate Emphasis on
Selected Reform Goals**

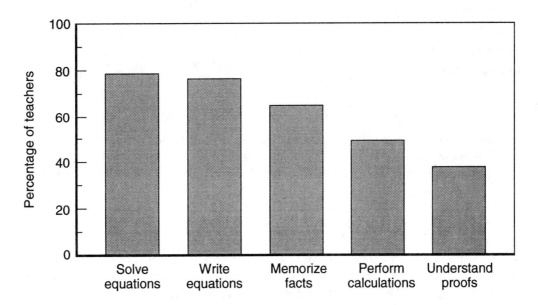

**Figure 5.2—Proportion of Teachers Reporting Major or Moderate Emphasis on
Traditional Goals**

Table 5.1

Instructional Goals Scales

	Reform	Traditional
Raising questions and formulating conjectures	+	
Judging the validity of arguments	+	
Finding examples and counterexamples	+	
Discovering generalizations	+	
Learning to represent problem structures in multiple ways (e.g., graphically algebraically, numerically)	+	
Representing and analyzing relationships using tables, charts, and graphs	+	
Conceiving and analyzing the effectiveness of different approaches to problem solving	+	
Applying mathematical models to real-world phenomena	+	
Designing a study or experiment	+	
Integrating math with other subjects	+	
Writing about mathematical ideas	+	
Solving problems for which there is no obvious method of solution	+	
Integrating different branches of mathematics (e.g., algebra, geometry) into a unified framework	+	
Memorizing facts, rules, and steps		+
Performing calculations with speed and accuracy		+
Solving equations		+
Writing equations to represent relationships		+
Understanding the nature of proof		+
Scale reliability (Cronbach's alpha)	0.86	0.37

We expected to see a positive correlation between reform goals and reform instructional activities and between traditional goals and traditional modes of teaching. The correlation between the reform goal scale and the reform instructional repertoire in Table 4.1 is strongly positive ($r = 0.75$), while the correlation between reform goals and the traditional teaching repertoire is negative ($r = -0.51$). However, traditional goals and traditional instructional activities are not correlated. The correlation between the traditional goal scale and the traditional instructional activities scale is negative ($r = -0.18$) and nonsignificant. The major reason is the lack of variation on these two scales: Two-thirds of the teachers reported a major or moderate emphasis on three or more of the five traditional goals, and 71 percent reported engaging in six or more of the nine traditional instructional strategies at least once or twice a week.

Our data confirm what Cohen and Peterson (1990) found in their study of the California mathematics framework—i.e., that even teachers who endorse curriculum reform and implement it in their own classrooms do so by integrating the new with the

Table 5.2

Instructional Goals Factor Matrix[a]

	Factor 1	Factor 2	Factor 3	Factor 4
Raising questions and formulating conjectures	0.81	−0.01	0.05	0.04
Understanding the nature of proof	0.77	−0.13	−0.13	0.05
Judging the validity of arguments	0.67	0.07	0.12	0.15
Finding examples and counterexamples	0.65	−0.02	0.13	−0.32
Increasing students' interest in math	0.61	0.05	0.13	−0.08
Discovering generalizations	0.51	0.31	0.14	0.02
Learning to represent problem structures in multiple ways (e.g., graphically, algebraically, numerically)	0.05	0.78	−0.01	−0.09
Writing equations to represent relationships	−0.18	0.60	0.13	−0.14
Representing and analyzing relationships using tables, charts, and graphs	−0.11	0.49	0.22	0.27
Conceiving and analyzing the effectiveness of different approaches to problem-solving	0.40	0.48	−0.23	−0.14
Memorizing facts, rules, and steps	−0.13	−0.46	0.14	−0.23
Applying mathematical models to real world phenomena	0.09	0.10	0.68	−0.01
Showing the importance of math in daily life	−0.06	−0.05	0.58	−0.28
Designing a study or an experiment	0.10	−0.12	0.48	0.39
Integrating math with other subjects	0.30	−0.09	0.47	0.01
Solving equations	0.00	0.30	0.12	−0.66
Writing about mathematical ideas	−0.08	0.28	0.22	0.59
Solving problems for which there is no obvious method of solution	0.04	0.27	−0.09	0.46
Integrating different branches of mathematics (e.g., algebra, geometry) into a unified framework	0.29	0.40	−0.11	0.10
Performing calculations with speed and accuracy	0.25	−0.01	0.07	−0.29
Eigenvalue	4.83	1.48	1.43	1.20

[a]Our exploratory analysis extracted five factors, four of which were substantially interpretable. The coefficients are from a promax rotation of the solution.

traditional. Although 46 percent of the teachers in our sample reported that they emphasize most of the reform goals in their teaching, only 12 percent of the sample engaged in four or more reform instructional activities at least once or twice a week. Seven teachers (10 percent of the sample) did report a moderate or major emphasis on nine or more reform goals and also reported using four or more reform-oriented instructional strategies at least once or twice or week. However, all but two of these teachers also use at least half of the traditional instructional strategies just as frequently. In other words, according to their own self-reports, few respondents in our sample rely on the instructional strategies that mathematics reformers espouse for advancing reform goals these teachers seem to accept. Furthermore, even the few respondents who might—by their own reports—be characterized as "reform teachers" use traditional teaching strategies as part of their instructional repertoires. Consistent with the implementation patterns that characterize the adoption of many classroom innovations, these teachers are layering new practices onto their existing ones.

CONSISTENCY BETWEEN THE SURVEYS AND THE ARTIFACTS

The level of consistency between teachers' self-reports on the surveys and coders' findings from the artifacts was considerably lower for goals than for either topic coverage or instructional strategies. The difficulty in interpreting data on instructional goals is further confounded when we compare teachers' self-reports with the artifact data coded from their assignments and exams. Table 5.3 shows the rate of agreement between the surveys and exams and between the surveys and assignments on the degree of emphasis teachers gave each of the instructional goals. The rate of agreement was slightly higher for assignments than for exams, perhaps because there were more data points from which to make inferences. On the whole, survey and artifact data were more consistent for traditional goals (4 of the 5 traditional goals had rates of agreement above the mean for the entire list) than for reform goals (4 of the 13 reform goals were above the mean).

The major source of the discrepancies could be traced to the coders' very different judgments about the amount of emphasis teachers were giving reform goals. Coders indicated that 75 percent of the teachers had given 12 of the 13 reform goals either a minor or no emphasis. This depiction of teachers' goals is generally consistent with the information on their exams and assignments that they themselves provided in their survey responses. For example, the survey data presented in Figure 4.2 indicate that only a small proportion of teachers' exams require students to describe how to solve problems, explain their reasoning, or apply concepts to unfamiliar situations. On the other hand, when asked to characterize their instruction through the lens of the goals they stress, teachers presented a very different picture. For only two of the reform goals (*writing about mathematical ideas* and *designing a study or experiment*) did an equally high proportion of teachers report a small emphasis, thus agreeing with the coders. As noted previously, nearly half reported giving a moderate or major emphasis to most reform goals, and for four goals, 75 percent or more reported doing so.[3]

These patterns—low levels of agreement between the survey and artifact data, more problems with reform than traditional goals, and teachers reporting a greater emphasis on reform goals than coders could detect—led us to reinterview a subsample of teachers. These subsequent interviews indicated that teachers had confounded frequency and importance. For example, one problem we discovered is that teachers interpreted the response options (*major, moderate, minor,* and *none*) for the goals

---

[3]The four goals to which 75 percent or more of the teachers reported giving a moderate or major emphasis are displayed in Figure 5.1 and listed in footnote 7 of Chapter Four.

Table 5.3

Instructional Goals: Consistency Between Surveys and Exams and Between Surveys and Assignments

	Exams		Assignments	
	Percent Direct Agreement	Percent Within One Survey Response Category	Percent Direct Agreement	Percent Within One Survey Response Category
Designing a study or experiment	53	90	58	92
Writing about mathematical ideas	42	82	44	89
Understanding the nature of proof	37	70	38	80
Performing calculations with speed and accuracy	30	87	30	87
Memorizing facts, rules, and steps	26	79	30	80
Solving equations	25	64	30	78
Representing and analyzing relationships using tables, charts, and graphs	23	62	29	71
Judging the validity of arguments	22	50	26	58
Solving problems for which there is no obvious method of solution	17	64	21	65
Writing equations to represent relationships	15	54	19	58
Integrating different branches of mathematics (e.g., algebra, geometry) into a unified framework	15	39	22	53
Learning to represent problem structures in multiple ways (e.g., graphically, algebraically, numerically)	13	49	20	61
Discovering generalizations	10	34	14	43
Applying mathematical models to real-world phenomena	10	50	12	52
Finding examples and counterexamples	10	36	11	49
Showing the importance of math in daily life	7	31	17	48
Integrating math with other subjects	7	48	18	64
Raising questions and formulating conjectures	6	29	12	42
Increasing students' interest in math	5	18	9	38
Conceiving and analyzing the effectiveness of different approaches to problem solving	3	26	8	33
Mean	19	53	23	62

item in different ways. This same set was used on the NELS-SFU questionnaire, and a variant of it has also been used on NAEP teacher surveys. But some teachers assumed that the underlying dimension was the frequency with which they undertook activities consistent with a particular goal, while others assumed that emphasis should be defined in terms of how important they considered a goal for their students' understanding, regardless of how often they undertook activities reflective of that goal. Other teachers combined frequency and importance in their assessment of emphasis.

Coders were instructed to base their judgments on the prevalence of tasks consistent with a particular goal—for reform goals, those tasks were identified from NCTM materials—and the goal's relative importance as compared with other objectives the teacher seemed to be stressing. The notion that some teachers might place a major emphasis on a goal but not incorporate it into many activities—e.g., by stressing it with great clarity and forcefulness at a few key points during the course—is not something that we could measure well with artifacts.

A second, and greater, problem is the different meanings that teachers ascribe to terms associated with the mathematics reform movement. Table 5.4 illustrates differing interpretations of an NCTM standard (1989: 75) that was included as one of the reform goals on the survey and that had the lowest level of agreement between the survey and the exam and assignment artifacts. At a general level, five of the six teachers interpreted the goal in a way consistent with its reform meaning—i.e., encouraging more than one solution method. But only the calculus teacher's discussion comes close to the notion of "conceiving," and most of the teachers seem to be interpreting problem-solving in a narrower sense of solving traditional mathematics problems, rather than strategies for solving real-world or nonroutine problems.

This example of disparate interpretations is by no means unique. The previous chapters reported problems with other reform-oriented terms. Not only did teachers have differing interpretations of these terms, but in a number of cases they reported not knowing at all what the phrases meant.

CONCLUSIONS

Our analysis suggests that instructional goals are too problematic to be validly measured through national surveys of teachers. The data are inconsistent not only with artifact data, but also with teachers' own self-reports on other survey items such as those describing their exam formats. These inconsistencies are difficult to interpret. The lack of a consistent relationship may stem from the different meanings teachers ascribe to terms associated with the mathematics reform movement. Or acknowledging the importance of particular goals may be a precursor to implementing instructional practices consistent with those objectives. Or, despite teachers' willingness to report candidly about their reliance on traditional instructional strategies, social desirability may be a factor in their discussions about their philosophy of teaching. There may be other plausible explanations for the disjuncture between teachers' reported goals and classroom practice, but at this point, we do not know which actually account for the inconsistencies. As a result, survey data on instructional goals cannot be unambiguously interpreted.

We therefore recommend that questions about teachers' instructional goals be deleted from national surveys. These items could be replaced with more detailed measures of topic coverage, thereby increasing the amount and quality of data on the

Table 5.4

Examples of Teachers' Interpretations of a Reform Goal

Item	Reform Definition	Teacher Interpretations[a]
Conceiving and analyzing the effectiveness of different approaches to problem solving	Helping students to be able to think of problem-solving strategies such as trial and error and other iterative methods, and to judge when to use a particular strategy	• "When we're working with signed numbers, I tell students you should go by the rules, but if you forget the rules, you can always figure out the answers logically. There are two methods: going by the rules or doing it logically." (General math teacher)
	Apply such strategies in solving "real world" and nonroutine problems	• "I do a lot of statement problems. I draw on the board." (Pre-algebra teacher)
		• "In Math A, we don't have too many different approaches. Now I see it as asking about what the teacher does." (Pre-algebra teacher)
		• "This goal is about how much discussion and presentation you do about alternative methods of solution. I don't consciously think of it; it naturally comes up." (Geometry teacher)
		• "This is more of a classroom activity where you talk about different approaches, especially if a student asks, 'Could I have solved the problem this way?'" (Math analysis teacher)
		• "When we come to new problems, I don't tell students anything, hoping they will ask good questions. Then I give them the background—the classical approach. I always encourage creative thinking, different ways to solve problems." (AP calculus teacher)

[a]In the group interviews, teachers were asked to tell us what types of activities they saw as representing a particular goal in the course they reported on in their survey.

most central aspect of curriculum, without greatly increasing respondent burden. At least in the short term, data on teachers' goals might be more effectively gathered through smaller, supplemental studies. Data might be collected as part of a validation study, so that teachers' self-reports could be compared with their instructional artifacts; or they might be collected using face-to-face, open-ended interviews, perhaps combined with classroom observations; or focus groups and similar strategies might be used to probe the meanings that teachers ascribe to different goals. Interpreting survey data about attitudes and beliefs is always difficult, but in the case of teachers' goals, the dangers of misinterpretation seem particularly high and appear to outweigh the value of obtaining information with a relatively inexpensive, broad-based method.

Chapter Six

DESIGN CHOICES FOR IMPROVED CURRICULUM INDICATORS

As curriculum assumes greater prominence on the education policy agenda, the demand for better indicators will continue. Three questions face those responsible for the design and operation of educational indicator systems:

- How will curriculum indicator data be used?

- How much do various users need to know about curriculum?

- What is the most effective strategy for collecting curriculum indicator data?

These are difficult questions to answer, and judgments about appropriate directions will be shaped as much by political values and resource constraints as by technical considerations. Nevertheless, the findings and conclusions of this study can help inform the decision process.

USES OF CURRICULUM INDICATOR DATA

The potential uses of curriculum indicator data could conceivably range from the kind of national snapshot now provided by NAEP, NELS, and similar surveys to the high-stakes applications implied in some proposed uses of OTL standards (McDonnell, 1995). An enhanced version of existing surveys could provide a reasonably valid depiction of the mathematics curriculum in this country, but it would have two major limitations: The characterization would be rather general, and it might not provide a very accurate picture of either teachers' intentions or practices with regard to curriculum reform. Still, it is possible to obtain sound information about the depth and breadth of course content and how it varies across courses and types of schools, and such information would provide a better indication of teachers' instructional repertoires than is currently available.

Despite the improvements that can be made in surveys over the next several years, we do not believe that the information collected will meet the necessary criteria for high-stakes uses. The data will still be too general to permit valid determinations about the alignment of individual schools with any type of content standards. Yet due process requires that valid and reliable measures of each school's curriculum be established before the school can be held accountable for its instructional activities. Given the measurement and interpretation problems we have identified, we do not believe that curriculum indicator data could meet such a legal standard in the near future.[1]   Therefore, the most appropriate uses for such data will continue to be informational uses.   Curriculum indicator data can provide a general picture of the distribution of OTL across different types of schools and students and it can chart overall trends in curricular practice, but it cannot serve as the basis for decisions that will have potentially serious consequences for schools and teachers.

INFORMATION NEEDS

The second question raises the issue of what should be included in the domain of curriculum. In this study, we focused on content coverage, instructional strategies, and goals—categories recommended in some form by most indicator designers. However, these categories are largely teacher-centered, and they do not directly measure the role of students in constructing knowledge. Measuring active student learning greatly complicates both the measurement and the data collection tasks and would likely necessitate more data than can be obtained from teacher surveys. However, it may soon be possible to consider another potentially large database as a source for curriculum indicators: The increased use of student portfolios by states and local districts for assessing students provides an opportunity to experiment with using such portfolios as sources of information about the nature of the teaching and learning process as well. Until now, research has focused on scoring student portfolios as measures of student achievement, but a parallel effort could focus on extracting data that might serve as indicators of the types of instructional strategies being used and students' role in those activities.

Even if curriculum is defined more narrowly in terms of the three categories we used and confined to indicators that can be effectively measured through teacher surveys, the level of detail desired within each of these categories can vary considerably. Given the relationship between students' curricular exposure and their achievement, as well as our study results showing that surveys can provide reasonably accurate measures of topic coverage, we recommend that future national surveys place a greater emphasis on such coverage.   Not only are the topics currently included on national teacher surveys too few and too general to provide a valid picture of OTL, the information they generate is virtually useless for understanding curricular trends. Future items on topic coverage should be tailored to specific course levels and should include more topics at a greater level of specificity. Our post–artifact-data-collection questionnaire is an example of such an enhanced survey.

Although we would accord it lower priority, we also recommend including a more comprehensive set of questions dealing with instructional strategies. Asking teachers

---

[1]Another issue that would arise if curriculum data were collected for high-stakes purposes relates to the quality of teachers' survey responses. We found few social-desirability problems in their responses. However, our surveys were administered under very low-stakes conditions. All the research showing that teachers change their behavior in response to the content and format of student assessments strongly suggests that under high-stakes conditions, teachers would likely bias their responses. They might find it in their interest to report responses consistent with policymakers' expectations, thus corrupting the information collected. As a result, validation studies would need to be conducted much more frequently than if the data were to be used only for informational purposes and no direct consequences were attached.

about a broader range of classroom practices would provide better information about the different ways they combine strategies and about how they integrate newer practices into their traditional repertoires. The findings from our study and a number of others indicate that teachers rely on only a few traditional strategies. Yet reformers and policymakers continue to expect that teachers will adopt a variety of instructional reforms. Whether that expectation will be met or not is an open question, but asking teachers about only a few traditional and a few reform practices ignores the reality of policy implementation. If teachers do adopt the instructional strategies advocated by reformers, it will be through a process of adaptation and layering (Darling-Hammond, 1990). If survey questionnaires do not contain a fairly comprehensive set of instructional practice items, it will be difficult to determine exactly what these hybrid repertoires look like or how consistent they are with reformist guidelines.

New survey items are also needed that can delve more deeply to identify variations in instructional strategies not adequately captured by broad survey categories such as *lecture* or *have small groups work on problems to find a joint solution.* We know from classroom observations that teachers have very different lecture styles, some of which are considerably more effective than others. Similarly, group work can vary considerably across classrooms, ranging from students leading each other in the learning process to completing worksheets individually while sitting with others. The successful design of a comprehensive and valid set of curriculum indicators requires that such distinctions—formerly measured only in intensive, small-scale studies—now be measured with survey data.

Current efforts to improve schooling through the setting of curricular standards that cover both content and instructional strategies make the design of indicator systems that strike the appropriate balance between measuring reform practices and measuring traditional ones a critical issue. A good indicator system allows for trend analyses by measuring the same core features of schooling similarly over time. However, an indicator system should also be able to measure progress consistent with the goals reflected in public policies and professional standards, even as they change in response to shifts in political priorities and the application of basic knowledge about teaching and learning to classroom practice. Given that the curriculum content and instructional practices in most classrooms are constant over time, the core of a curriculum indicator system should include a stable set of measures for which repeated data are collected. These would include most of the items that we have labeled "traditional" in our analysis and that form the core of most teachers' instructional strategies.

A second set of measures could include items associated with the reforms currently on the policy and practice agenda. Given the stability of instructional practice in the face of numerous reform fads, we would recommend that this set of reform-based measures be kept relatively small and that new measures be included only where both policy and professional practice standards evidence a strong, long-term commitment to the instructional approaches embodied in the new measures. The time and expense involved in indicator development and data collection are not warranted unless there is a reasonable expectation that the reform practices being measured will be implemented in a large number of classrooms.

We recognize that our recommendations for greater emphasis on curriculum content and instructional strategies would require additional time for survey administration and hence increase respondent burden. The tradeoff between improved data quality and respondent burden is a particular problem in the case of national surveys used to collect a variety of different data from the same respondents. However, because teachers' instructional goals cannot be validly measured through survey data, the additional burden associated with an enhanced survey on topic coverage and instructional strategies could be reduced somewhat by eliminating those items dealing with instructional goals.

DATA COLLECTION STRATEGIES

Decisions about use and scope will largely determine data collection strategies. Our findings suggest three areas of possible investment. The first, improving the design of national surveys, has already been discussed. In addition to changing the relative emphasis accorded different aspects of curriculum, a number of suggested changes in item wordings and response option scales were outlined in previous chapters. These changes can be implemented quite cost-efficiently.

A second area of future investment is in-depth studies on small samples of teachers and classrooms to monitor changes in mathematics teaching. These studies would use techniques that can measure instructional processes with greater subtlety than is possible through surveys. More complete, nuanced data about such issues as teachers' understanding of reform goals and their different uses of reform strategies could be used to interpret survey results and to improve the design of future surveys.

The final area for future investment is the one that has been the primary focus of this study: We believe that the kind of validation study we have piloted should be integrated into the design of curriculum indicator systems. The primary, and most pressing, reason for validation studies is the current reform context. Proposed changes in curriculum content and instructional practice mean that the language of mathematics teaching is in flux, and teachers do not share a common understanding of key terms. The effect is likely to be either a serious misinterpretation of survey results or an inability to interpret them at all. Problematic survey items can be clarified through the use of more precise definitions and concrete examples. However, as we noted in the case of instructional strategies, so few teachers have adopted the new approaches that it is difficult to test alternative wordings of survey questions or experiment with new measures. Consequently, until language and practice have stabilized, validation studies (perhaps combined with in-depth case studies and focus-group interviews) will need to be an integral part of curriculum indicator systems.

Although current interest in curriculum reform and hope for its widespread implementation provide the primary rationale for validation studies, such studies would still be needed even in more stable times. By collecting detailed data from multiple sources over shorter periods of time, validation studies can provide benchmarks against which to judge both the validity and reliability of survey data. It is only with such data that we can determine whether teachers are reporting reliable estimates of topic coverage and whether their characterizations of exams and assignments are accurate. Such independently collected information not only helps in interpreting survey data but also identifies sources of measurement error and informs the design of future surveys.

A validation study need not be conducted every time a national survey is administered. We would recommend conducting one only when a new survey effort is begun—e.g., at the beginning of a longitudinal study like NELS or when major design changes are implemented in the NAEP teacher survey. The validation study could be conducted prior to the first administration of the survey as part of the design phase. A validation study would be required for a national survey only every five years or so and would increase the cost of the survey by approximately 10 to 20 percent.

Although we would recommend several modifications in the procedures used in our pilot study, we believe that the basic structure is sound. The instructional artifacts worked well as benchmarks and, despite some obvious limitations, were easily collected from teachers. Although coding artifacts to extract information comparable to that collected from the surveys was difficult, we now have a template that can be improved upon and replicated quite easily. Given what we have learned from the pilot study, we are confident that the level of agreement among raters can be increased. The coding specifications can be made more precise, and the coding process can be organized so that coders' work is reviewed more frequently through a moderation process that identifies discrepant judgments and makes appropriate adjustments. The coding of instructional artifacts will never be as reliable as, for example, the scoring of open-ended test items, because the type and mix of material is unstandardized across teachers. Nevertheless, we believe that use of the survey categories as the basis for a content analysis of the artifacts and close monitoring of the coding process can result in high-quality benchmark data.

To make valid comparisons across courses, future validation samples will need to be somewhat larger—probably about twice as large as the sample used for this pilot study. However, given that there is less variation in the curriculum of upper-level courses such as calculus and policy concerns about OTL are greatest in lower-level courses, one option might be to concentrate the study's focus on courses at or below the algebra II level. Particular emphasis might be placed on lower-level courses such as pre-algebra and on those that integrate topics across traditional course categories.

The similarity of our findings about teachers' instructional practices to those from larger, nationally representative samples suggests that our smaller sample is generally reflective of high school mathematics teaching. However, to avoid idiosyncrasies that might characterize the teacher force in only one or two states, future validation studies should include teachers from a larger number of states. For example, the proportion of California mathematics teachers who have a college major in mathematics is considerably below the national average (44 percent in 1991, as compared with a national average of 69 percent) (Blank and Gruebel, 1993).[2] With the modifi-cations outlined, the basic approach used in this pilot study should serve as an effec-tive template for future validation studies.

Over the past decade, the quality of education indicators has steadily improved, par-ticularly indicators of school and classroom processes. The "black box" that charac-terized older input-output models has been replaced with an increasingly compre-hensive set of indicators that can report national trends in school organization and curriculum. But the failure to validate these indicators has remained a problem. Be-cause items are typically transferred from one survey to another with no attempts at validation, the extent to which they measure how students are actually taught is vir-tually unknown. This study represents a first step toward ensuring that curriculum indicators are valid and reliable measures of the instruction occurring in the nation's classrooms.

---

[2]We focused on California because the state has innovative curriculum frameworks, which we assumed would lead to more reform-oriented teachers being included in our sample. However, like many others, we underestimated the difficulty of implementing the frameworks and the length of time implementation would take.

SURVEY INSTRUMENTS

VALIDATING NATIONAL CURRICULUM INDICATORS

INITIAL TEACHER SURVEY

This questionnaire asks for some initial information about the goals, content, and instructional activities in the class that has been chosen for the RAND/UCLA study on validating curriculum indicators. This information, along with the instructional materials you will be providing, will help in describing students' educational experiences.

The survey includes questions about characteristics of the class, teaching strategies, curriculum content, and general information about your teaching experience.

Please mark your responses directly on the questionnaire. Place it in the envelope with your class assignments for the first week, and return it to RAND.

THANK YOU FOR YOUR CONTRIBUTION TO THIS STUDY.

Class Information

---

1.   Identity Code: _____

2.   Class Title: _____

3.   How many students are enrolled in this class?

No. of Students: ☐☐

4.   How many students in this class are from minority racial/ethnic groups (e.g., Black, Hispanic, Asian)? (If unsure, give your best estimate.)

No. of Students: ☐☐

5.   Which of the following best describes the level this class is considered to be?

(Circle One)

Remedial 1

General 2

Voc/Tech/Business 3

College Prep/Honors 4

AP 5

6.   Which of the following best describes the achievement level of the students in this class compared with the average student in this school?

(Circle One)

Higher achievement levels 1

Average achievement levels 2

Lower achievement levels 3

Widely differing achievement levels 4

7.   Approximately how much homework do you typically assign each day to this class?

Minutes: ☐☐

8.   How often do you do each of the following with homework assignments?

(Circle One Number on Each Line)

	Never	Some of the Time	Most of the Time	All of the Time
a. Keep records of who turned in the assignment	1	2	3	4
b. Return assignments with grades or corrections	1	2	3	4
c. Discuss the completed assignment in class	1	2	3	4

9.   Approximately how many minutes per week does this class meet regularly (not including lab periods)?

Minutes: ☐☐

10.   Approximately how may minutes per week does this class have lab sessions? (If there is no lab, enter "00.")

Minutes: ☐☐

11.   Indicate about what percent of class time is spent in a typical week doing each of the following with this class.

(Circle One Number on Each Line)

	None	<10%	10-24%	25-49%	50-74%	75-100%
a. Providing instruction to the class as a whole	1	2	3	4	5	6
b. Providing instruction to small groups of students	1	2	3	4	5	6
c. Providing instruction to individual students	1	2	3	4	5	6
d. Maintaining order/disciplining students	1	2	3	4	5	6
e. Administering tests or quizzes	1	2	3	4	5	6
f. Performing routine administrative tasks (e.g., taking attendance, making announcements, etc.)	1	2	3	4	5	6
g. Conducting lab periods	1	2	3	4	5	6

12.   How often do you use the following teaching methods or media?

(Circle One Number on Each Line)

	Never/ Rarely	1-2 Times a Month	1-2 Times a Week	Almost Everyday	Everyday
a. Lecture	1	2	3	4	5
b. Use computers	1	2	3	4	5
c. Use audio-visual material	1	2	3	4	5
d. Have teacher-led whole-group discussion	1	2	3	4	5
e. Have students respond orally to questions	1	2	3	4	5
f. Have student-led whole-group discussions	1	2	3	4	5
g. Have students work together in cooperative groups	1	2	3	4	5
h. Have students complete individual written work	1	2	3	4	5
i. Have students give oral reports	1	2	3	4	5

13.   Indicate the importance you give to each of the following in setting grades for students in your classes (excluding special education students).

(Circle One Number on Each Line)

	Not Important	Somewhat Important	Very Important
a. Achievement relative to the rest of the class	1	2	3
b. Absolute level of achievement	1	2	3
c. Individual improvement or progress over past performance	1	2	3
d. Effort	1	2	3
e. Class participation	1	2	3
f. Completing homework assignments	1	2	3
g. Consistently attending class	1	2	3

```
┌─────────────────────────────────────────────┐
│              For Math Teachers Only           │
└─────────────────────────────────────────────┘
```

Those teaching science classes should *SKIP TO QUESTION 16* on the following page.

14.   **In this math class, how much emphasis do you give to each of the following objectives?**

(Circle One Number on Each Line)

		None	Minor	Moderate	Major
a.	Understanding the nature of proofs	1	2	3	4
b.	Memorizing facts, rules, and steps	1	2	3	4
c.	Learning to represent problem structures in multiple ways (e.g. graphically, algebraically, numerically, etc.)	1	2	3	4
d.	Integrating different branches of math (e.g., geometry, algebra) into a unified framework	1	2	3	4
e.	Conceiving and analyzing effectiveness of multiple approaches to problem solving	1	2	3	4
f.	Performing calculations with speed and accuracy	1	2	3	4
g.	Showing importance of math in daily life	1	2	3	4
h.	Solving equations	1	2	3	4
i.	Raising questions and formulating conjectures	1	2	3	4
j.	Increasing students' interest in math	1	2	3	4

15.   **Have you taught or reviewed the following topics in this math class during this year?** (If you have reviewed and taught an item as new content, mark #3 only.)

(Circle One Number on Each Line)

		No, but it was was taught previously	Yes, but I reviewed it only	Yes, but I taught it as new content	No, but I will teach or review it later this year	No, topic is beyond the scope of this course
a.	Integers	1	2	3	4	5
b.	Patterns and functions	1	2	3	4	5
c.	Linear Equations	1	2	3	4	5
d.	Polynomials	1	2	3	4	5
e.	Properties of geometric figures	1	2	3	4	5
f.	Coordinate Geometry	1	2	3	4	5
g.	Proofs	1	2	3	4	5
h.	Trigonometry	1	2	3	4	5
i.	Statistics	1	2	3	4	5
j.	Probability	1	2	3	4	5
k.	Calculus	1	2	3	4	5

For Science Teachers Only

Those teaching math classes only should *SKIP TO THE SECTION MARKED* Teacher Background

16.   In this science class, how much emphasis do you give to the following objectives?

(Circle One Number on Each Line)

	None	Minor	Moderate	Major
a. Increasing students' interest in science	1	2	3	4
b. Learning and memorizing scientific facts, principles, and rules	1	2	3	4
c. Learning scientific methods	1	2	3	4
d. Preparing students for future study in science	1	2	3	4
e. Developing problem solving/inquiry skills	1	2	3	4
f. Developing skills in lab techniques	1	2	3	4
g. Learning about applications of science to environmental issues	1	2	3	4
h. Showing importance of science in daily life	1	2	3	4

17.   How often do you do each of the following activities in this science class?

(Circle One Number on Each Line)

	Never/ Rarely	1-2 Times a Month	1-2 Times a Week	Almost Everyday	Everyday
a. Have students do an experiment or observation individually or in small groups	1	2	3	4	5
b. Demonstrate an experiment or lead students in systematic observations	1	2	3	4	5
c. Require students to turn in written reports on experiments or observations	1	2	3	4	5
d. Discuss current issues and events in science	1	2	3	4	5
e. Have students use computers for data collection and analysis	1	2	3	4	5
f. Use computers for demonstrations/simulations	1	2	3	4	5
g. Have students give oral reports	1	2	3	4	5
h. Have students independently design and conduct their own science projects	1	2	3	4	5
i. Discuss career opportunities in scientific and technological fields	1	2	3	4	5
j. Discuss controversial inventions and technologies	1	2	3	4	5

18. **For biology teachers:** Have you taught or reviewed the following topics in this Biology class during this year? If you have reviewed and taught an item as new content, mark #3 only.

(Circle One Number on Each Line)

		No, but it was was taught previously	Yes, but I reviewed it only	Yes, but I taught it as new content	No, but I will teach or review it later this year	No, topic is beyond the scope of this course
a.	Cell structure and function	1	2	3	4	5
b.	Genetics	1	2	3	4	5
c.	Diversity of life	1	2	3	4	5
d.	Metabolism and regulation of the organism	1	2	3	4	5
e.	Behavior of the organism	1	2	3	4	5
f.	Reproduction and development of the organism	1	2	3	4	5
g.	Human biology	1	2	3	4	5
h.	Evolution	1	2	3	4	5
i.	Ecology	1	2	3	4	5

19. **For physics teachers:** Have you taught or reviewed the following topics in this Physics class during this year? If you have reviewed and taught an item as new content, mark #3 only.

(Circle One Number on Each Line)

		No, but it was was taught previously	Yes, but I reviewed it only	Yes, but I taught it as new content	No, but I will teach or review it later this year	No, topic is beyond the scope of this course
a.	Forms and sources of energy	1	2	3	4	5
b.	Forces, time, motion	1	2	3	4	5
c.	Molecular/nuclear physics	1	2	3	4	5
d.	Energy/matter transformations	1	2	3	4	5
e.	Sound and vibrations	1	2	3	4	5
f.	Light	1	2	3	4	5
g.	Electricity and magnetism	1	2	3	4	5
h.	Solids/fluids/gases	1	2	3	4	5

Teacher Background and Experience

1.   **What is your sex?**

Male................................. 1

Female 2

2.   **Which best describes you?**

Asian or Pacific Islander............................. 1

Hispanic, regardless of race 2

Black, not of Hispanic origin 3

White, not of Hispanic origin 4

American Indian or Alaskan Native 5

3.   **What is the year of your birth?**

(Last 2 digits):   ☐☐

4.   **Counting this year, how many years in total have you taught at either the elementary or secondary level?**

K-6:   ☐☐

7-12:   ☐☐

5.   **Counting this year, how many years in total have you taught in this school?**

Years: ☐☐

6.   **What academic degree(s) do you hold?**

(Circle All That Apply)

No degree 0   ---> SKIP TO Q8

Associate degree 1   ---> SKIP TO Q8, if only degree

Bachelor's 2

Master's 3

Education specialist or professional
diploma at least one year of work
beyond master's level 4

Doctorate 5

First professional degree (e.g., M.D., D.D.S.) 6

7.   **What were your major and minor fields of study for your bachelor's degree?**

(Circle All That Apply)

		Major	Minor
a.	Education	1	1
b.	Mathematics	2	2
c.	Natural/physical sciences	3	3
d.	Life/biological sciences	4	4
e.	Computer science	5	5
f.	Foreign language	6	6
g.	English	7	7
h.	History (or social science)	8	8
i.	Other	9	9

8.   Circle the number beside any of the following subjects which you have taught this year.

(Circle All That Apply)

MATHEMATICS

General Math 01

Pre-Algebra 02

Algebra I 03

Algebra II 04

Geometry 05

Trigonometry 06

Pre-Calculus... 07

Calculus 08

Consumer/Business Math 09

AP Calculus 10

Other Math 11

SCIENCE

General Science... 12

General Physical Science 13

Earth Science... 14

Principles of Technology.............................. 15

Biology 16

Chemistry... 17

Physics... 18

AP Science.. 19

Other Science 20

OTHER

Computer Science.. 21

Other non-math, non-science
course 22

Please describe _____

Date completed: ☐☐ / ☐☐ / ☐☐

    MO   DAY   YR

Thank you for your assistance.

Please return this survey in the same envelope
with your first week's instructional materials.

VALIDATING NATIONAL CURRICULUM INDICATORS

MATHEMATICS TEACHER SURVEY

As part of the larger study to examine different ways of measuring curriculum trends in schools, this questionnaire asks you to report on the goals, content, and instructional activities in the class for which you have been providing us with your instructional materials. Specifically, it asks about the curriculum content covered, the teaching strategies and instructional practices used, and your goals, objectives and general beliefs about the way mathematics should be taught to this class The information you provide, along with other data already collected, is intended to describe students' educational experiences. Also, because this study will inform future efforts, space is provided at the end of the questionnaire for your comments on any problems or recommendations.

Please MARK YOUR RESPONSES DIRECTLY ON THE QUESTIONNAIRE. Place it in the envelope with your instructional materials for this week, and return it to RAND.

THANK YOU FOR YOUR CONTRIBUTION TO THE STUDY.

Form I   9/17/92

Class Characteristics

Please provide the following information about the specific class listed below:

Designated class: _____

1. How many students are in this class?   _____ Total

    _____ Females

    _____ Males

2. How many of the students in this class are in the following grade levels? (Sum should equal total number of students given above.)

    a. 9th grade   _____
    b. 10th grade   _____
    c. 11th grade   _____
    d. 12th grade   _____

3. Which of the following best describes the achievement level of the students in this class in comparison to the average student in this school? (Circle one.)

    This class consists primarily of students with:

Higher achievement levels	1
Average achievement levels	2
Lower achievement levels	3
Widely differing achievement levels	4

4. How many of the students in this class are of limited or non-English speaking ability?

    _____

Form I   9/17/92

5. How many of the students in this class are members of the following ethnic/racial groups? (Sum should equal total given above in question 1.)

    a. American Indian or Alaskan Native   _____

    b. Asian or Pacific Islander   _____

    c. Hispanic, regardless of race   _____

    d. Black (not of Hispanic origin)   _____

    e. White (not of Hispanic origin)   _____

    f. Other (specify) _____   _____

6. How many students in this class are likely to do the following in the future? (Sum should equal total given above in question 1.)

    a. Attend a 4-year college   _____

    b. Attend a 2-year college/technical school   _____

    c. End formal education with high school   _____

    d. Not graduate from high school   _____

Curriculum Coverage

Please answer the following questions about the content you taught this class.

7. What was the primary text used in this class?

    Title: _____

8. What chapters do you plan to cover by the end of this semester?

    Chapters: _____

    How closely did you follow the text? (Describe your use of the text below.)

    _____

    _____

9. What additional chapters do you plan to cover over the course of this year?

    Chapters: _____

Form I   9/17/92

You will find a list of topics on this page and the next 2 pages. Please respond to the following questions for each of the topics listed.

10. Have you taught or reviewed the following topics during this year in this class? (Circle your response.)

    1 = No, but it was taught previously.

    2 = Yes, but I reviewed it only.

    3 = Yes, I taught it as new content (includes new topics which will be reviewed later).

    4 = Not yet, but I will teach or review it later this school year.

    5 = No, topic is beyond the scope of this course or not in the school curriculum.

11. Indicate the approximate number of periods devoted to each topic below. If you focus on a topic for 10 or 15 minutes on a given day, count that as a period. If you will teach or review a topic later this year, indicate the number of periods you anticipate spending on the topic. (Circle your response.)

    1 = None (zero)

    2 = One or two periods

    3 = Three to five periods

    4 = Six to ten periods

    5 = More than two weeks but less than one month (11 to 20 class periods)

    6 = One month or more (more than 20 periods)

		Topics:	10. Taught or reviewed? No, Taught previously / Yes, Reviewed Only / Yes, New content / Not yet, Later in year / No, Beyond course					11. Periods on topic? 0 Periods / 1-2 Periods / 3-5 Periods / 6-10 Periods / 11-20 Periods / > 20 Periods					
	a.	Patterns and functions	1	2	3	4	5	1	2	3	4	5	6
	b.	Estimation	1	2	3	4	5	1	2	3	4	5	6
	c.	Proportional reasoning	1	2	3	4	5	1	2	3	4	5	6
	d.	Proofs	1	2	3	4	5	1	2	3	4	5	6
	e.	Tables and charts	1	2	3	4	5	1	2	3	4	5	6
	f.	Graphing	1	2	3	4	5	1	2	3	4	5	6
	g.	Math modeling	1	2	3	4	5	1	2	3	4	5	6
*	h.	Ratios, proportions, and percents	1	2	3	4	5	1	2	3	4	5	6
*	i.	Conversions among fractions, decimals and percents	1	2	3	4	5	1	2	3	4	5	6
*	j.	Laws of exponents	1	2	3	4	5	1	2	3	4	5	6
*	k.	Square roots	1	2	3	4	5	1	2	3	4	5	6
	l.	Polynomials	1	2	3	4	5	1	2	3	4	5	6
*	m.	Linear equations	1	2	3	4	5	1	2	3	4	5	6
	n.	Slope	1	2	3	4	5	1	2	3	4	5	6
*	o.	Writing equations for lines	1	2	3	4	5	1	2	3	4	5	6
*	p.	Inequalities	1	2	3	4	5	1	2	3	4	5	6
	q.	Quadratic equations	1	2	3	4	5	1	2	3	4	5	6
*	r.	Applications of measurement formulas (e.g. area, volume)	1	2	3	4	5	1	2	3	4	5	6
	s.	Properties of geometric figures	1	2	3	4	5	1	2	3	4	5	6
*	t.	Pythagorean Theorem	1	2	3	4	5	1	2	3	4	5	6

			10. Taught or reviewed?					11. Periods on topic?					
			No, Taught previously	Yes, Reviewed Only	Yes, New content	Not yet, Later in year	No, Beyond course	0 Periods	1-2 Periods	3-5 Periods	6-10 Periods	11-20 Periods	>20 Periods
	u.	Coordinate geometry	1	2	3	4	5	1	2	3	4	5	6
	v.	Probability	1	2	3	4	5	1	2	3	4	5	6
	w.	Statistics	1	2	3	4	5	1	2	3	4	5	6
*	x.	Distance, rate, time problems	1	2	3	4	5	1	2	3	4	5	6
	y.	Growth and decay	1	2	3	4	5	1	2	3	4	5	6
**	z.	Transformational geometry	1	2	3	4	5	1	2	3	4	5	6
**	aa.	Logarithms	1	2	3	4	5	1	2	3	4	5	6
**	bb.	Conic sections	1	2	3	4	5	1	2	3	4	5	6
**	cc.	Trigonometry	1	2	3	4	5	1	2	3	4	5	6
**	dd.	Polar coordinates	1	2	3	4	5	1	2	3	4	5	6
**	ee.	Sequences	1	2	3	4	5	1	2	3	4	5	6
**	ff.	Complex numbers	1	2	3	4	5	1	2	3	4	5	6
**	gg.	Vectors	1	2	3	4	5	1	2	3	4	5	6
**	hh.	Matrices and matrix operations	1	2	3	4	5	1	2	3	4	5	6
**	ii.	Calculus	1	2	3	4	5	1	2	3	4	5	6
**	jj.	Limits	1	2	3	4	5	1	2	3	4	5	6
**	kk.	Integration	1	2	3	4	5	1	2	3	4	5	6
**	ll.	Fundamental counting principle, permutations, combinations	1	2	3	4	5	1	2	3	4	5	6
**	mm.	Measures of dispersion (range variance, standard deviation, etc.)	1	2	3	4	5	1	2	3	4	5	6
**	nn.	Discrete math (e.g., Euler circuits, directed graphs, trees)	1	2	3	4	5	1	2	3	4	5	6

* indicates topic in Form I only.
** indicates topic in Form II only.

12. For each item below, please indicate the types of <u>student understanding</u> you expect from the majority of this class by the end of the course. (Circle the highest number that applies.)

1 = Recognizes/knows the rule or principle
2 = When given the rule or principle, is able to use it
3 = Knows when and how to apply the rule or principle
4 = Can both apply the rule or principle and explain why it works as it does
5 = Not applicable—rule or principle beyond the scope of this class

a. Division by zero is not allowed: $\frac{a}{0}$ is undefined for all numbers a   1   2   3   4   5

b. In a plane, the sum of the angle measures in any triangle is 180   1   2   3   4   5

c. The area of a triangle: $A = \frac{1}{2}bh$ 1   2   3   4   5

d. The Pythagorean Theorem   1   2   3   4   5

e. The slope of a vertical line is undefined   1   2   3   4   5

f. The distance formula: $d = \sqrt{(x_2-x_1)^2 + (y_2-y_1)^2}$ 1   2   3   4   5

h. If $\frac{a}{b} = \frac{c}{d}$, then $ad = bc$ 1   2   3   4   5

h. $(a+b)^2 = a^2 + 2ab + b^2$ 1   2   3   4   5

i. The product rule for exponents: $a^m \cdot a^n = a^{m+n}$ 1   2   3   4   5

j. The square root of a negative number is not a real number   1   2   3   4   5

k. The log of a negative number is not defined   1   2   3   4   5

l. A continuous function need not be differentiable   1   2   3   4   5

Instructional Practices

Please answer the following questions about the organization, teaching strategies and instructional practices you used with this class.

13. How often do you use each of the following instructional strategies with this class? (The strategy need not take the entire class period.)

		Almost every day	Once or twice a week	Once or twice a month	Once or twice a semester	Never
a.	Lecture	1	2	3	4	5
b.	Have students respond orally to questions on subject matter	1	2	3	4	5
c.	Have student-led whole group discussions	1	2	3	4	5
d.	Have teacher-led whole group discussions	1	2	3	4	5
e.	Correct and/or review homework in class	1	2	3	4	5
f.	Demonstrate working an exercise at the board	1	2	3	4	5
g.	Have students work exercises at the board	1	2	3	4	5
h.	Have students work individually on written assignments or worksheets in class	1	2	3	4	5
i.	Have students give oral reports	1	2	3	4	5
j.	Administer a test (full period)	1	2	3	4	5
k.	Administer a quiz	1	2	3	4	5
l.	Use manipulatives (e.g., conic section models) to demonstrate a concept	1	2	3	4	5

(Continued on next page.)

Form I   9/17/92

	Almost every day	Once or twice a week	Once or twice a month	Once or twice a semester	Never
m. Discuss career opportunities in mathematics	1	2	3	4	5
n. Have small groups work on problems to find a joint solution	1	2	3	4	5
o. Have whole class discuss solutions developed in small groups	1	2	3	4	5
p. Have students practice or drill on computational skills	1	2	3	4	5
q. Have students work on problems for which there is no obvious method of solution	1	2	3	4	5
r. Have students represent and analyze relationships using tables and graphs	1	2	3	4	5
s. Have students use calculators to solve exercises or problems	1	2	3	4	5
t. Have students use computers to solve exercises or problems	1	2	3	4	5
u. Have students respond to questions or assignments that require writing at least a paragraph	1	2	3	4	5
v. Have students keep a mathematics journal	1	2	3	4	5
w. Have students read textbooks or supplementary materials	1	2	3	4	5
x. Have students work with manipulatives	1	2	3	4	5
y. Have students work on next day's homework in class	1	2	3	4	5
z. Summarize main points of today's lesson	1	2	3	4	5
aa. Have students work on projects in class	1	2	3	4	5

Form I   9/17/92

14. Indicate what percent of class time is spent in a typical week doing each of the following with this class. (Circle one on each line. The total need not sum to 100%.)

	Percent					
	None	< 10	10-24	25-49	50-74	75-100
a. Providing instruction to the *class* as a whole	1	2	3	4	5	6
b. Providing instruction to *small groups* of students	1	2	3	4	5	6
c. Providing instruction to *individual students*	1	2	3	4	5	6
d. Maintaining order/disciplining students	1	2	3	4	5	6
e. Administering tests or quizzes	1	2	3	4	5	6
f. Performing routine administrative tasks (e.g., taking attendance, making announcements, etc.)	1	2	3	4	5	6
g. Conducting lab periods	1	2	3	4	5	6

Evaluation and Grading Practices

15. On the tests, quizzes, and exams you administer to this class, about what percent of the items are of the following types? (Total should equal 100% in each column.)

	Tests and Quizzes	Final Exam
a. Multiple-choice	______%	______%
b. Short-answer	______%	______%
c. Essay	______%	______%
d. Open-ended problems (i.e., where students generate their own solutions)	______%	______%
e. Other (specify) ____________	______%	______%

16. On the tests and quizzes you administer to this class, about what <u>percent of the items</u> are of the following types? (Total need <u>not</u> sum to 100%.)

    a. Items that require students to recognize or recall definitions or concepts   _____%

    b. Items that require the use of algorithms to solve problems   _____%

    c. Items that require students to describe how to solve problems   _____%

    d. Items that require students to explain their reasoning   _____%

    e. Items that require the application of concepts or principles to different or unfamiliar situations   _____%

    h. Items that require a critique or analysis of a suggested solution to a problem   _____%

    i. Other (specify) _____   _____%

17. On the tests and quizzes you administer to this class, about what <u>percent of the items</u> are of the following types? (Total need <u>not</u> sum to 100%.)

    a. Exercises or problems that are minor variations of homework or class exercises or problems   _____%

    b. Exercises or problems with more than one possible answer   _____%

    c. Exercises or problems with more than one possible approach   _____%

    d. Exercises or problems that require more than one step to reach a solution   _____%

    e. Items that require the use of tabular or graphical data   _____%

18. What will be the approximate distribution of final student grades in this class? (Total should equal number of students in the class.)

    A's _____

    B's _____

    C's _____

    D's _____

    F's _____

Homework Policies and Practices

19. Approximately how much homework do you typically assign each day to this class?

    _____ minutes

20. How often do you do each of the following with homework assignments?

		Never	Some of the time	Most of the time	All of the time
a.	Keep records of who did or who turned in the assignment	1	2	3	4
b.	Return assignments with grades or corrections	1	2	3	4
c.	Discuss the completed assignment in class	1	2	3	4

21. How frequently do you assign each of the following types of homework?

		Almost every day	Once or twice a week	Once or twice a month	Once or twice a semester	Never
a.	Reading the text or supplementary materials	1	2	3	4	5
b.	Doing exercises or problems from the text	1	2	3	4	5
c.	Doing exercises or problems from worksheets	1	2	3	4	5
d.	Writing definitions of concepts	1	2	3	4	5
e.	Applying concepts or principles to different or unfamiliar situations	1	2	3	4	5
f.	Solving problems for which there is no obvious method of solution	1	2	3	4	5
g.	Gathering data, conducting experiments, working on projects	1	2	3	4	5
h.	Preparing oral reports	1	2	3	4	5
i.	Preparing written reports	1	2	3	4	5
j.	Extending results established in class (e.g., deriving or proving new results)	1	2	3	4	5
k.	Keeping a journal	1	2	3	4	5
l.	Solving applied problems (e.g., finding the amount of water needed to fill a pool)	1	2	3	4	5
m.	Explaining newspaper/magazine articles	1	2	3	4	5

Form I   9/17/92

Materials, Equipment and Technology

22.   How frequently do you use the materials and equipment listed below with this class?

	Almost every day	Once or twice a week	Once or twice a month	Once or twice a semester	Never
a. Graph paper	1	2	3	4	5
b. Protractors, rulers, or compasses	1	2	3	4	5
c. A-V equipment (e.g., film projector, VCR, cassette, TV)	1	2	3	4	5
d. Overhead projector	1	2	3	4	5
f. Four-function calculator	1	2	3	4	5
g. Scientific calculator	1	2	3	4	5
h. Graphing calculator	1	2	3	4	5
i. Other (specify)	1	2	3	4	5

_____

Form I   9/17/92

Goals, Objectives and Teacher Beliefs

23. How much emphasis do you give to each of the following objectives in this class?

		No	Minor	Moderate	Major
				Emphasis	
a.	Understanding the nature of proof	1	2	3	4
b.	Memorizing facts, rules and steps	1	2	3	4
c.	Learning to represent problem structures in multiple ways (e.g., graphically, algebraically, numerically)	1	2	3	4
d.	Integrating different branches of mathematics (e.g., algebra, geometry) into a unified framework	1	2	3	4
e.	Conceiving and analyzing the effectiveness of different approaches to problem solving	1	2	3	4
f.	Performing calculations with speed and accuracy	1	2	3	4
g.	Showing the importance of math in daily life	1	2	3	4
h.	Solving equations	1	2	3	4
i.	Raising questions and formulating conjectures	1	2	3	4
j.	Increasing students' interest in math	1	2	3	4
k.	Integrating math with other subjects	1	2	3	4
l.	Finding examples and counterexamples	1	2	3	4
m.	Judging the validity of arguments	1	2	3	4
n.	Discovering generalizations	1	2	3	4
o.	Representing and analyzing relationships using tables, charts and graphs	1	2	3	4
p.	Applying mathematical models to real-world phenomena	1	2	3	4
q.	Writing about mathematical ideas	1	2	3	4
r.	Designing a study or experiment	1	2	3	4
s.	Writing equations to represent relationships	1	2	3	4
t.	Solving problems for which there is no obvious method of solution	1	2	3	4

24.   Indicate the degree to which you emphasized the following strategies with this class.

	No	Minor	Moderate	Major
		Emphasis		
a. Students received a good deal of practice to become competent at mathematics.	1	2	3	4
b. I routinely justified the mathematical principles and procedures used.	1	2	3	4
c. I corrected student errors immediately.	1	2	3	4
d. Students were provided frequent opportunities to discover mathematical ideas for themselves.	1	2	3	4
e. I gave step-by-step directions for applying algorithms and procedures.	1	2	3	4
f. Students were provided opportunities to apply mathematics to real-world situations.	1	2	3	4
g. Students developed their own methods of solving math problems.	1	2	3	4
h. Students were frequently expected to discover generalizations and principles on their own.	1	2	3	4
i. Students learned to solve problems in different ways.	1	2	3	4
j. Students were required to memorize and apply rules.	1	2	3	4
k. Students learned there is usually a rule to apply when solving a math problem.	1	2	3	4
l. Students received step-by-step directions to aid in solving problems.	1	2	3	4

25. There are a variety of ways in which teachers describe their role in helping their students learn
     mathematics. Statements A through D represent several possibilities. Please read these statements,
     then answer the question below about your role.

     A: "I mainly see my role as a facilitator. I try to provide opportunities and resources for my students
         to discover or construct mathematical concepts for themselves."

     B: "I think I need to provide more guidance than that. Although I provide opportunities for them to
         discover concepts, I also try to lead my students to figure things out by asking pointed questions
         without telling them the answers."

     C: "I emphasize student discussion of math in my classroom. We talk about concepts and problems
         together, exploring the meaning and evaluating the reasoning that underlies different strategies.
         My role is to initiate and guide these discussions."

     D: "That's all nice, but my students really won't learn math unless you go over the material in a
         detailed and structured way. I think it's my job to explain, to show students how to do the work,
         and to give them practice doing it."

     Which statement best typifies your conception of your role in helping students in this class learn math?
     (Place an X on the continuum below to indicate your role.)

                    A   B   C   D

26. Below are two pairs of statements. Each pair represents opposite ends of a continuum in curriculum
     approaches. After reading a pair of statements, place an X on the line between that pair indicating
     where you would place your approach with this class.

                        Pair 1: My primary goal is to help students

     A: learn mathematical   B: achieve a deeper conceptual
     terms, master computational   understanding of mathematics
     skills and solve word problems

                    A _____ B

                        Pair 2: In this mathematics class, I aim for

     A: in-depth study of selected   B: comprehensive coverage
     topics and issues, even if it   even if it means sacrificing
     means sacrificing coverage   in-depth study

                    A _____ B'

Form I   9/17/92

The following questions concern the questionnaire itself. Please provide this information so that we might improve the questionnaire for future use.

27.   Were any of the questions confusing or unclear?

_____ No

_____ Yes   If Yes, please list the question number and describe the source of confusion.

Number   Source of Confusion

_____   _____

_____   _____

_____   _____

_____   _____

_____   _____

_____   _____

_____   _____

_____   _____

_____   _____

28.   Use the space below to describe any other problems or make any recommendations about the questionnaire.

_____

_____

_____

_____

_____

_____

_____

_____

Daily Log

Name_____   Course_____

Date_____   School_____

1.   List the content covered in this class period by briefly describing it or providing examples.

TOPICS

2.   What modes of instruction did you use? (Check all that apply.)

Lecture to entire class   _____
Demonstrate an exercise at the board   _____
Use manipulatives or audio-visual materials
   to demonstrate a concept   _____
Demonstrate an experiment   _____
Lead question and answer session   _____
Work with small groups   _____
Work with individual students   _____
Correct or review homework   _____
Other (please specify)_____

3.   What activities did students engage in during this period? (Check all that apply.)

Listen and take notes   _____
Work exercises at board   _____
Work individually on written assignments or worksheets   _____
Work with other students   _____
Work with manipulatives   _____
Use calculators   _____
Respond to questions   _____
Discuss topics from lesson   _____
Work on next day's homework   _____
Work on computer   _____
Conduct lab experiment   _____
Write lab report   _____
Other (please specify)_____

Comments:_____

_____

_____

_____

_____

Blank, R. K., and Gruebel, D. (1993) *State indicators of science and mathematics education.* Washington, DC: Council of Chief State School Officers.

Burstein, L. (Ed.) (1993). *The IEA study of mathematics III: Student growth and classroom processes.* New York: Pergamon.

California Department of Education (1992). *Mathematics framework for California public schools.* Sacramento, CA: Author.

Cohen, D. K., and Peterson, P. L. (1990). Special issue of *Educational Evaluation and Policy Analysis,* 12 (3), 233–353.

Council of Chief State School Officers (1994). *Inventory of state education accountability reports, indicator reports, and report cards.* Washington, D.C.: Author.

Darling-Hammond, L. (1990). Instructional policy into practice: "The power of the bottom over the top." *Educational Evaluation and Policy Analysis,* 12 (3), 339–347.

Freeman, D. J., Kuhs, T. M., Porter, A. C., Floden, R. E., Schmidt, W. H., and Schwille, J. B. (1983). Do textbooks and tests define a national curriculum in elementary school mathematics? *Elementary School Journal,* 83 (5), 501–513.

Gamoran, A., and Nystrand, M. (1991). Background and instructional effects on achievement in eighth-grade English and social studies. *Journal of Research on Adolescence,* 1 (3), 277–300.

Goodlad, J. I. (1984). *A place called school.* New York: McGraw-Hill.

Goodling, B. (1994, March 23). A failed policy about inputs. *Education Week,* XIII(26), 36.

Harp, L. (1994, May 18). The plot thickens: The real drama behind the Kentucky education reform act may have just begun. *Education Week,* 20–25.

Jones, L. V., Davenport, E. C., Bryson, A., Bekhuis, T., and Zwick, R. (1986). Mathematics and science test scores as related to courses taken in high school and other factors. *Journal of Educational Measurement,* 23 (3), 197–208.

Kifer, E. (1993). Opportunities, talents and participation. In L. Burstein (Ed.), *The IEA study of mathematics III: Student growth and classroom processes* (pp. 279–307). New York: Pergamon.

McDonnell, L. M. (1995). Opportunity-to-learn as a research concept and a policy instrument. *Educational Evaluation and Policy Analysis.*

McDonnell, L. M., Burstein, L., Ormseth, T., Catterall, J. M., and Moody, D. (1990). *Discovering what schools really teach: Designing improved coursework indicators.* Santa Monica, CA: RAND.

McKnight, C. C., Crosswhite, F. J., Dossey, J. A., Kifer, E., Swafford, J. O., Travers, K. J., and Cooney, T. J. (1987). *The underachieving curriculum: Assessing U.S. school mathematics from an international perspective.* Champaign, IL: Stipes Publishing.

McLaughlin, M. W. (1990). The RAND Change Agent Study revisited: Macro perspectives and micro realities. *Educational Researcher*, 19(9), 11–16.

Merl, J. (1994, May 6). Furor continues to build over state's CLAS exams. *Los Angeles Times*, A1, 18.

Mullis, I. V. S., Dossey, J. A., Owen, E. H., and Phillips, G. W. (1991). *The state of mathematics achievement: NAEP's 1990 assessment of the nation and the trial assessment of the states* (OERI Rep. No. 21-ST-04). Princeton, NJ: Educational Testing Service.

Mullis, I. V. S., Jenkins, F., and Johnson, E. (1994). *Effective schools in mathematics: Perspectives from the NAEP 1992 assessment* (OERI Rep. No. 23-RR-01). Washington, D.C.: U.S. Government Printing Office.

Murnane, R. J., and Raizen, S. A. (1988). *Improving indicators of the quality of science and mathematics education in grades K–12.* Washington, DC: National Academy Press.

National Council of Teachers of Mathematics (1989). *Curriculum and evaluation standards for school mathematics.* Reston, VA: Author.

National Council of Teachers of Mathematics (1991). *Professional standards for teaching mathematics.* Reston, VA: Author.

National Council on Education Standards and Testing (1992). *Raising standards for American education.* Washington, DC: U.S. Government Printing Office.

National Research Council (1989). *Everybody counts: A report to the nation on the future of mathematics education.* Washington, DC: National Academy Press.

National Study Panel on Education Indicators (1991). *Education counts: An indicator system to monitor the nation's educational health.* Washington, DC: U.S. Government Printing Office.

Oakes, J. (1985). *Keeping track: How schools structure inequality.* New Haven, CT: Yale University Press.

Oakes, J., and Carey, N. (1989). Curriculum. In R. J. Shavelson, L. M. McDonnell, J. Oakes (Ed.) *Indicators for monitoring mathematics and science education: A sourcebook.* Santa Monica, CA: RAND.

O'Day, J. A., and Smith, M. S. (1993). Systemic reform and educational opportunity. In S. H. Fuhrman (Ed.), *Designing coherent education policy* (pp. 250–313). San Francisco: Jossey-Bass.

OERI State Accountability Study Group (1988). *Creating responsible and responsive accountability systems.* Washington, DC: U.S. Department of Education.

Owens, M. R. (1994, March 23). The name of the camel is truth. *Education Week, XIII(26),* 35–36.

Porter, A. C. (1991). Creating a system of school process indicators. *Educational Evaluation and Policy Analysis, 13(1),* 13–29.

Porter, A. C., Kirst, M. W., Osthoff, E. J., Smithson, J. L., and Schneider, S. A. (1993). Reform up close: *An analysis of high school mathematics and science classrooms.* University of Wisconsin-Madison, Wisconsin Center for Education Research, School of Education.

Raizen, S. A., and Jones, L. V. (Eds.) (1985). *Indicators of precollege education in science and mathematics: A preliminary review.* Washington, DC: National Academy Press.

Ravitch, D. (1995). *National standards in American education.* Washington, DC: Brookings.

Riley, R. W. (1994). The Goals 2000: Educate America Act. Providing a world-class education for every child. In J. F. Jennings (Ed.), *National Issues in education: Goals 2000 and School-to-Work* (pp. 3–25). Bloomington, IN: Phi Delta Kappa International, and Washington, D.C.: The Institute for Educational Leadership.

Rothman, R. (1993, April 7). 'Delivery' standards for schools at heart of new policy debate. *Education Week,* 21.

Schmidt, W. H., Wolfe, R. G., and Kifer, E. (1993). The identification and description of student growth in mathematics achievement. In L. Burstein (Ed.), *The IEA study of mathematics III: Student growth and classroom processes* (pp. 59–75). New York: Pergamon.

Shavelson, R. J., McDonnell, L. M., and Oakes, J. (Eds.) (1989). *Indicators for monitoring mathematics and science education: A sourcebook.* Santa Monica, CA: RAND.

Shavelson, R., McDonnell, L. M., Oakes, J., and Carey, N., with Picus, L. (1987). *Indicator systems for monitoring mathematics and science education.* Santa Monica, CA: RAND.

Smith, M. S., and Scoll, B. W. (1995). The Clinton human capital agenda. *Teachers College Record*, 96 (3), 389–404.

Travers, K. J. (1993). Overview of the longitudinal version of the second international mathematics study. In L. Burstein (Vol. Ed.), *The IEA study of mathematics III: Student growth and classroom processes* (pp. 1–27). New York: Pergamon.

Travers, K. J., Garden, R. A., and Rosier, M. (1988). Introduction to the study. In D. F. Robitaille and R. A. Garden (Eds.), *The IEA study of mathematics II: Contexts and outcomes of school mathematics* (pp. 1–16). New York: Pergamon.

Travers, K. J., and Westbury, I. (Eds) (1989). *The IEA study of mathematics I: Analysis of mathematics curricula* . New York: Pergamon.

Weiss, I. (1994). *A profile of science and mathematics education in the United States: 1993.* Chapel Hill, NC: Horizon Research, Inc.

Wittrock, M. C. (Ed.) (1985). *Handbook of research on teaching* (3rd ed.). New York: Macmillan.